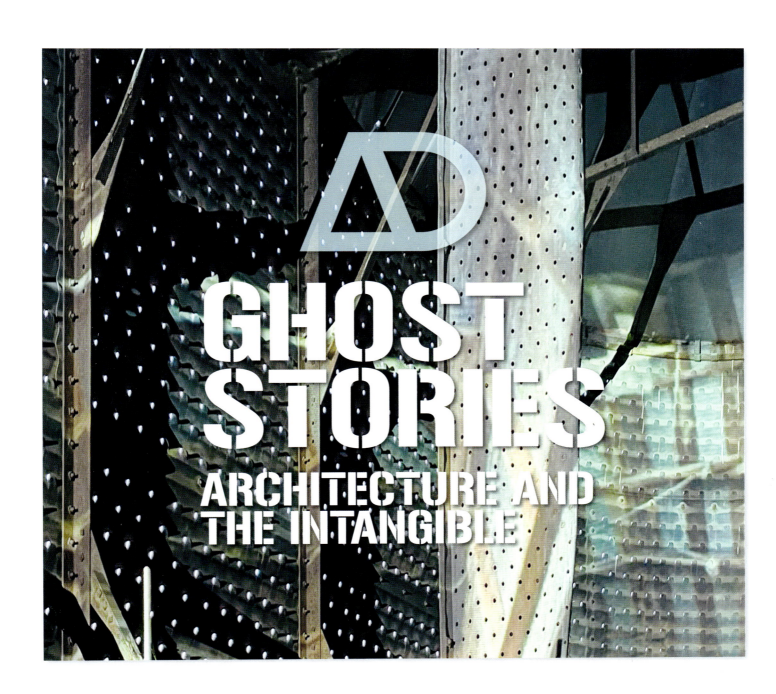

GHOST STORIES
ARCHITECTURE AND THE INTANGIBLE

Guest-edited by Peter J Baldwin

04 | Vol 94 | 2024

GHOST STORIES
ARCHITECTURE AND THE INTANGIBLE

04/2024

About the Guest-Editor 5
Peter J Baldwin

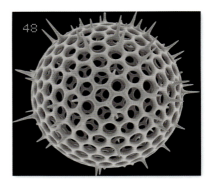

Introduction
I Ain't Afraid Of No Ghosts … 6
Peter J Baldwin

Syncopated Chronologies 16
Architectural Conservation and
Spectral Documentation
Cameron Stebbing

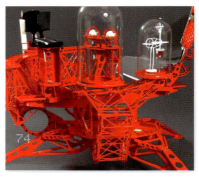

Imaging Uncertainty 26
Layers of Time and Meaning
in a Sacred Space
Eva Menuhin

Haunted Houses 34
Architecture and Large
Language Models
Chris Speed

**Phantoms of a
Five-Day Forest** 40
Kirsty Badenoch

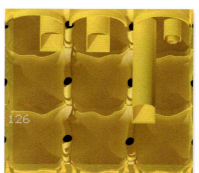

ISSN 0003-8504   ISBN 978 1 394 18508 5   Guest-edited by **Peter J Baldwin**

Designing Absence — 48
The Invisible Bridge and the Ghost Barn
Ian Ritchie

Solid Shadows — 58
Presencing Memory, Manifesting Memorial
Peter J Baldwin

Ghost Horizons — 64
Scaffold and Syntax
Oliver G Goché and Peter P Goché

Chasing Paradoxical Shadows — 74
Nat Chard

Diaphanous Bodies — 84
A Hauntology of the Mediating Image
Peter J Baldwin

All Visualisations Have Crooked Tales/Tails — 92
Perry Kulper

A Tailored Reality — 102
Inside In Here
Ifigeneia Liangi and Daniel Dream

Digital Ectoplasm and the Infinite Architecture of the Fulldome — 110
Mike Phillips

Piranesi — 118
An Unsettling World of Architecture
Mark Morris

Hard Spirits — 126
Architectural Apparitions in Hayao Miyazaki's *Spirited Away*
Michael Chapman

From Another Perspective
Beyond the Realms of Death — 134
Neil Spiller

'Evident throughout human history, the relationship between architecture and the immaterial has long been established'
— Peter J Baldwin

Contributors — 142

Editorial Offices
John Wiley & Sons
9600 Garsington Road
Oxford
OX4 2DQ

T +44 (0)18 6577 6868

Editor
Neil Spiller

Managing Editor
Caroline Ellerby
Caroline Ellerby Publishing

Freelance Contributing Editor
Abigail Grater

Publisher
Todd Green

Production Editor
Elizabeth Gongde

Design and Prepress
Artmedia, London

Printed in the United Kingdom
by Hobbs the Printers Ltd

Front cover
Nat Chard, Institute of Paradoxical Shadows Research Field with mischievous floating shadows, 2023. © Nat Chard

Inside front cover
Mark West, *Campfire Girl – A Ghostly Figure the Emergence of a Body*, 2016. © Mark West

Page 1
Peter P Goché, Granary, Napier, Iowa, 2023.
© Peter P Goché

EDITORIAL BOARD

Denise Bratton
Paul Brislin
Mark Burry
Helen Castle
Nigel Coates
Peter Cook
Kate Goodwin
Edwin Heathcote
Brian McGrath
Jayne Merkel
Peter Murray
Mark Robbins
Deborah Saunt
Patrik Schumacher
Jill Stoner
Ken Yeang

ARCHITECTURAL DESIGN

July/August 2024
Volume 94
Issue 04

Journal Customer Services
For ordering information, claims and any enquiry concerning your journal subscription please go to www.wileycustomerhelp.com/ask or contact your nearest office.

Americas
E: cs-journals@wiley.com
T: +1 877 762 2974

Europe, Middle East and Africa
E: cs-journals@wiley.com
T: +44 (0)1865 778 315

Asia Pacific
E: cs-journals@wiley.com
T: +65 6511 8000

Japan
(for Japanese-speaking support)
E: cs-japan@wiley.com
T: +65 6511 8010

Visit our Online Customer Help available in 7 languages at www.wileycustomerhelp.com/ask

Print ISSN: 0003-8504
Online ISSN: 1554-2769

All prices are subject to change without notice.

Identification Statement
Periodicals Postage paid at Rahway, NJ 07065. Air freight and mailing in the USA by Mercury Media Processing, 1850 Elizabeth Avenue, Suite C, Rahway, NJ 07065, USA.

USA Postmaster
Please send address changes to Architectural Design, John Wiley & Sons Inc., c/o The Sheridan Press, PO Box 465, Hanover, PA 17331, USA

Rights and Permissions
Requests to the Publisher should be addressed to:
Permissions Department
John Wiley & Sons Ltd
The Atrium
Southern Gate
Chichester
West Sussex PO19 8SQ
UK

F: +44 (0)1243 770 620
E: Permissions@wiley.com

All Rights Reserved. No part of this publication may be reproduced, stored in a retrieval system or transmitted in any form or by any means, electronic, mechanical, photocopying, recording, scanning or otherwise, except under the terms of the Copyright, Designs and Patents Act 1988 or under the terms of a licence issued by the Copyright Licensing Agency Ltd, 5th Floor, Shackleton House, Battle Bridge Lane, London SE1 2HX, without the permission in writing of the Publisher.

△D is published bimonthly and is available to purchase as individual volumes at the following prices.

Individual copies:
£29.99 / US$45.00
Mailing fees for print may apply

ABOUT THE
GUEST-EDITOR

PETER J BALDWIN

Peter J Baldwin is a registered and chartered architect, artist and educator known for his experimental drawings and critical commentary on contemporary representational practices. He currently teaches at Loughborough University, where he holds the role of Lecturer (Assistant Professor) in Architecture, and serves as a validation visiting panel member for the Architects Registration Board.

For the past 17 years Peter has engaged with the profession formally and informally as a student, practitioner and educator, teaching and lecturing at schools across the UK. As an educator he is committed to developing the andragogic practices, representational methods and conceptual frameworks needed to support and foster the development of dexterous, generous architectural practitioners who are prepared for the challenges facing both the profession and the wider context in which it operates. To this end, in 2016 he established Studio C, an experimental design unit at the University of Lincoln, which seeks to question the role and nature of architecture in a post-postmodern context, and the emerging consequences of digitisation. The unit explores the ethics, agency and drivers for design in a society ever-more absorbed by its dual existence. Growing beyond its academic origins, Studio C has become a porous entity, an extended peer-mentoring community and an emerging research laboratory.

Peter's own research has in recent years become increasingly preoccupied with the role and practice of drawing and its capacity as an environment for speculation. Charting a largely unmapped disciplinary territory between the documentation of spatial effect and artistic arte[fact], the work exploits the generative potential of non-traditional modes of architectural representation in an attempt to initiate a conversation between process, image and representation. He was invited to exhibit at the Yale School of Architecture as part of the 'In Memoriam' exhibition (2019), and his research has been published in △ *Radical Architectural Drawing* (May/June 2022), *DRAWING: Research, Theory, Practice* (Intellect Books, 2022) and △ *A Sublime Synthesis: Architecture and Art* (September/October 2023). He also edited Professor Bryan Cantley's latest book *Speculative Coolness* (Routledge, 2023).

Most recently, Peter's work has focused on the reconceptualisation of architectural drawing as a host for the intangible through the conception of a spectral third – an interstitial state poised at 'the moment of becoming' that occupies the threshold between interiority and exteriority within Derrida's double system of meaning. It is this fascination with the ephemeral that, combined with the inspirations and powerful provocations that occur as the inevitable consequence of a long and salubrious lunch with the goodly Professor Neil Spiller, gave rise to this issue of △. △

Text © 2024 John Wiley & Sons Ltd. Image © James Smith

I Ain't Afraid Of No Ghosts ...

INTRODUCTION

PETER J BALDWIN

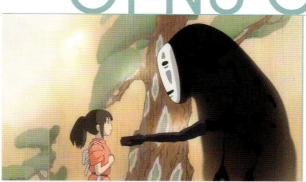

Ghosts [...] violate conceptual thinking based on dichotomous oppositions. They are neither fully present nor absent [...]
— Jeffrey Andrew Weinstock, *Spectral America: Phantoms and the National Imagination*, 2004[1]

From our earliest myths and legends to the more contemporary phantasmagoria that have emerged from the growing synthesis between the physical and the virtual, ghosts have long haunted our cultural consciousness and collective imaginations. Representing a state between states, they are a supreme challenge to thinking based upon binary oppositions. The appearance of the spectre is portentous, simultaneously manifesting our hopes and dreams and projecting our conscious and subconscious fears, oft heralding turbulence and calamity. Unbound by terrestrial notions of causation and causality, they offer warnings but also the chance for redemption. Perhaps that is why they are so prevalent in our collective imagination in the present day? Popularised in film and fiction, the uncanny and the ethereal are enjoying something of a renaissance.

Framing the spectral as a deconstructive gesture that undermines the fixedness and certainty of binary logics,[2] this issue of 𝔻 taps into that contemporary resurgence and our enduring fascination with the ethereal and uncanny, offering insights and speculations on the renewed conceptual relevance of latency, contingency and indeterminacy in the face of emerging architectural opportunities, spatial potentials and the unprecedented challenges facing both the discipline and the context within which it must now operate. Heralding architecture's long-overdue 'spectral (re)turn', its articles set out to provoke and inform a greater level of critical debate and awareness of the disjunctions between contemporary practice's predisposition towards the instrumental and material, historical understandings of the communicative capacities of architecture and pop-cultural depictions of architecture as a mediating link between the physical and the intangible.

Captain Hubert C Provand,
The Brown Lady of Raynham Hall,
1936
opposite: Haunted by the presence of the ghost or the spectre, the architectural object is intimately entwined with our conceptualisation of the unknown and ethereal, acting as a bridge between worlds or temporalities. Captured, quite accidentally, during a now apocryphal photoshoot for *Country Life* magazine at Raynham Hall in Norfolk, UK, in 1936, the 'Brown Lady' is purportedly Dorothy Walpole – wife of Charles Townshend, 2nd Viscount Townshend – who died at the Hall in 1726.

Hayao Miyazaki,
Film still of No-Face and Shen in *Spirited Away*,
2001
above: Ghosts, or spirits, are curiously global and enduring in their cultural presence, found within the traditions of societies many hundreds of years and thousands of miles apart, from medieval Europe to present-day Japan. More curious still is the near-universal re-emergence and growing presence of the spectre within popular media and our collective imagination in the first decade after the millennium. In both contemporary and historical depictions, the spectre is frequently cast as an agent of disclosure, carrying messages, warnings or 'gifts' from other places and times.

Conditions of (Un)Certainty

Evident throughout human history, the relationship between architecture and the immaterial has long been established. From the Neolithic temples of Göbekli Tepe in present-day Turkey, to the soaring spires of the Gothic cathedrals of 12th-century France, to more contemporary marvels of emotive experience such as Daniel Libeskind's Jewish Museum in Berlin (2001), architecture is understood as a mediating mechanism, a bridge between the tacit and the tangible, a vessel for our narratives and rituals and a repository for our myths and legends.[3]

As we hurtle through the 21st century however, technological innovation, smart infrastructures and emergent spatial typologies are overlaying the strata of centuries of accumulated sociocultural ephemera. Our myths, legends and hauntological flotsam and jetsam of society are competing with escalating political tensions and cultural turmoil, social unrest and the progressive collapse of our social institutions, each vying for our attention. As our worlds collide and our realities merge, we are drawn, inexorably, into a super-positioning, a condition of simultaneous experience, in which the tensions, disjunctions and contradictions of our existence become ever more profound.

At the same time as the very fabric of our world is changing in these ways, so too is our principal source of understanding it. With the emergence of 'media culture', our growing dependence on the digital infosphere has fundamentally shifted our approach to the acquisition of knowledge and the development of ideas and has profoundly altered our perception of events, conditions and contexts, shaping our views and interactions with the world around us. We no longer trust our own intuitions and instincts; it is not necessary to sense or feel; it has become sufficient to witness. Seeing has replaced believing.

Despite our hunger for 'awareness', as the 21st century unfolds, the instrumentality of modern thought has progressively distanced us from the catastrophic fallout of our post-industrial patterns of consumption. We are now facing the very real consequences of this hubris: the climate crisis, ecological and social catastrophe that are capitalism's last tango.

Daniel Libeskind, 'Congregations', *Theatrum Mundi*, 1985

above: In his seminal book *Theatrum Mundi*, the Polish-American architect Daniel Libeskind offers the premonition of a future city under siege by an unknown infection. While the exact nature of this infection is never overtly stated, careful study of the looped set of 12 abstract drawings and the text that make up this project reveals that, whatever it may be, the infection occupies a dualistic, virtual state, evading explicit categorisation, yet the repercussions of its presence are clearly felt.

Mathew Emmett, *The Martyrdom of St Sebastian II*, 2022

opposite: Occupying a spectral interstitiality, somewhere between immersive projection and physical environment, experimental architect and artist Mathew Emmett's work, inspired in this case by earlier artists' depictions of the martyrdom of St Sebastian, might be considered a contemporary baroque. Here the body of the saint becomes volatilised, rendered insubstantial by technological means, pierced by shafts of data rather than arrows.

Object(ification)

Paradoxically in an age characterised by dematerialisation and growing uncertainty, architecture has, in recent years, forfeited its fundamental purpose, becoming increasingly preoccupied with purely physical and quantifiable aspects of design. Consequently, as a discipline and profession we are coming to experience something of an identity crisis.

Driven by risk-averse practices, increasingly didactic teaching methods and the proliferation of the object and its image, our epistemological (and representational) models have come to favour grounding, clarity and explicit information, presuming the triumph of science and history over that of myth, language and art. In the face of this growing dominance of object-oriented ontological constructs and the emerging instrumentality of contemporary thinking, architectural thought and conceptualisation retreated into certainty, forcing the conditions of latency, uncertainty and indeterminacy – essential to the manifestation of architectonic and imaginative potential[4] – to the margins of the page.

With the loss of imaginative ambiguity, 21st-century architectural thought has succumbed to inertia, nostalgia and retrospection. Lost in a pervasive soup of postmodern -isms and -ologies, we are failing to move beyond the conceptualisations and tropes of the latter half of the 20th century: practically anything produced in the last decade could have been produced near the turn of the millennium. We have lost the capacity to conceptualise a world radically different to the one in which we currently live; there is no leading edge of innovation any more.

In our post-digital, visual-centric, (multi)media-saturated society, there is an overt lack of critical discourse addressing the implications of this loss. This has created a chasm between normative practice, with its pressures, and the need for a fundamental recalibration of disciplinary operations, leaving us ill-equipped to deal with the uncertain and indeterminate nature of the conditions and spaces that are the emerging consequences of capitalism.

As our world becomes increasingly indeterminate, unstable and uncertain, as practitioners and students of architecture we must begin to reconsider architecture's relationship with the latent and insubstantial.

Soyun Lim,
Stereoscopic Hallway, The Embassy of the Anonymous,
X-25 postgraduate unit,
Bartlett School of Architecture,
University College London (UCL),
2023

Not only associated with architecture, haunting has also often been linked to objects and artefacts. Bartlett student Soyun Lim's postgraduate project The Embassy of the Anonymous explored the totemic artefact as a source of fear and comfort, mediating a personal, emotional paradox that is often associated with the spectre.

A Spectral (Re)Turn
While there can be little doubt that the Bulgarian Nobel laureate Elias Canetti was correct in his assertions that we have witnessed the departure of the historic and consequently symbolic,[5] then what of Baudrillard's assertion that we turn towards the object?[6] What if the architectural object itself begins to disappear? It is perhaps at this point of maximum entropy, of maximal dissolution, that the spectral, the hauntological remains of our pasts, our futures, of cultures, arts, language and myth begin to manifest once more, offering an ephemeral reminder of that which has (already) left us, but for which we still yearn, for which we cry out, these cultural equivalents, which whisper to us from the cusp of sensory confusion, the siren songs of lost lovers …

First described by noted philosopher Jacques Derrida in his highly controversial *Spectres of Marx* (1993),[7] hauntology is posited as both a parallel conceptual construct and alternative logic to its more accepted and established near homonym ontology. Yet whilst ontological thinking prioritises being and presence in its attempts to categorise and define relational structuring, hauntology conceptualises the spectral as a paradoxical third state that shadows the dichotomy, evading distinct categorisation. Simultaneously present and absent, the fluidic figure of the spectre manifests as a deconstructive gesture, disclosed through perceptual layering and palimpsestic thinking.

Freed from the linear constraints and traditional notions of progress(ion), the atemporal agency of hauntology allows the contemporaneous consideration of a range of ideas and heterogeneous fragments, framed as a generative multiplicity, a promiscuous plurality that permits free mixing of imagination, emergent technologies and the persistence of elements from our sociocultural pasts. Perhaps, then, hauntology and its spectral agency offer the means to develop strategies, methods and frameworks through which we can begin to operate in our increasingly indeterminate conditions.

An Ethereal Ensemble
Owing to the inherent tension and (un)certainty within any work that aligns itself with the ethereal, the spectral speculations that are gathered hereafter actively resist definitive categorisation. Instead, a warp of more concrete architectural themes of space, place, method and technology are juxtaposed with a weft of history, science, art, language and myth, the sociocultural constants defined by the German anthropologist Ernst Cassirer,[8] offering multiple mutable combinations of readings as the articles flit from one state to another.

We begin our spectral journey with a form of ending as University of Huddersfield and University of Lincoln alumnus Cameron Stebbing explores notions of authenticity through the syncopated chronologies and the ethical and aesthetic tensions inherent within conservation architecture, before moving to the more documentative efforts of the Captivate: Spatial Modelling Research Group (based at the University of Greenwich in London), explored by author and editor Eva Menuhin, who offers us a poetic insight into the manifestation of hidden histories and revealed truths through the process of LiDAR scanning. Contrasting with this, Chris Speed, Professor of Design for Regenerative Futures at RMIT University in Melbourne, offers us a warning of the inherent biasing of these historic datasets, as he explores notions of erasure and the propensity for underlying rules sets to emerge regardless of how they are manipulated and used.

Artist, architect and Head of Research at the spatial design agency Periscope, Kirsty Badenoch explores the spectral syntax of centuries of land use (some might say abuse) of Beinn Eighe, the UK's first state-owned and -operated nature reserve, leaving us with open questions as to how architects might surrender to this ghostliness.

Ian Ritchie of the architectural practice ritchie*studio offers answers to some of these questions through the subtle rereading and nuanced reinterpretation of the implicit history of the site of his latest project, Ghost Barn. Continuing this trajectory, I recall a recent visit to renowned British sculptor Michael Sandle's London studio, considering how our own histories haunt our creative acts and actions. By contrast, architect and educator Peter P Goché and artist Oliver G Goché explore appropriated and repurposed spaces, reading those ghosts that haunt such structures and photographically projecting new imaginings onto and into them.

Hippolyte Baraduc,
The Church of Sacré-Cœur,
1895

The discovery of X-rays in December 1895 by the German scientist Wilhelm Conrad Röntgen sparked an epistemological crisis: for the first time since the dawning of enlightenment, the veracity of vision as a medium of absolute disclosure was proven false. This sparked a wave of explorations of various photographic imaging techniques, including those of the French physician and parapsychologist Hippolyte Baraduc, who developed various processes and techniques, including the 'Psychicone', to capture images of the electro-vital forces that he believed to be responsible for ghostly auras, psychic activity and ultimately the human soul.

Naturally projection, photography and in particular X-rays share a kinship with the spectre, and Nat Chard, Professor of Experimental Architecture at the Bartlett School of Architecture, University College London (UCL), shares his latest experiments with stereoscopic imaging: the creation of a spectral and paradoxical floating shadow. Building on this uncertainty, my own article explores the creation of ambiguity within my latest series of drawings, explaining both the inspiration and the situation the work seeks to undermine.

Perry Kulper, Professor of Architecture at Taubman College, University of Michigan, reveals his own hauntological framework, composed of tall tales and tangents, through an exploration of his latest work *Gifting, Ghosting & Gigabytes*, shown at the Chicago Architecture Biennial in the autumn of 2023. Venturing further into a world of tall tales, we enter the fantastical phantasmagoria of the Night Kitchen studio where Bartlett tutors Ifigeneia Liangi and Daniel Dream weave their spatial narratives. Diving deeper into the reaches indeterminate of narrative constructs, Professor of Interdisciplinary Arts and Director of Research at the creative technology open research lab i-DAT, Mike Phillips leads us into the immersive virtual realm of the fulldome and its many spectral inhabitants. A similarly haunted realm, that of award-winning author Susanna Clarke's novel *Piranesi* (2020), is the next topic of investigation, its haunted confines and uncanny chambers laid bare by the probing gaze of Mark Morris, Director of Teaching and Learning at London's Architectural Association (AA) School of Architecture. Finally we return in some senses to our point of departure with our last article, as Chair of Architecture at Western Sydney University Michael Chapman offers his own forensic reconstruction, this time of the architecture in Hayao Miyazaki's film *Spirited Away* (2001), exploring the embedded memories and mythical traces of the folklore of Japan.

An Ethereal Age

Whether we like it or not, the spectral (re)turn is upon us, and the ethereality of the coming age will mark a new chapter in architecture's long romance with the incorporeal. It is up to us as current and future generations of practitioners to rediscover our lost futures, those spaces of spectral uncertainty and imaginative ambiguity that will provide the means to develop new practices and positions from which to address our contemporary uncertainties. This △ issue is intended to catalyse those conversations, to challenge, invite and inspire readers to (re)consider the implications of the spectral, latent and ephemeral within their own work, for, as Derrida so aptly reminds us, 'the future belongs to Ghosts'.[9] △

Notes
1. Jeffrey Andrew Weinstock, *Spectral America: Phantoms and the National Imagination*, University of Wisconsin Press (Madison, WI), 2004, p 7.
2. *Ibid*
3. See CJ Lim and Ed Liu, *Short Stories: London in Two and a Half Dimensions*, Routledge (Abingdon), 2011, pp 6–7.
4. See Dalibor Vesely, *Architecture in the Age of Divided Representation*, MIT Press (Cambridge, MA), 2006, pp 7–8.
5. Elias Canetti, *The Human Province*, Seabury Press (New York), 1978, p 69.
6. Jean Baudrillard, *Fatal Strategies*, Semiotext(e) (Pasadena, CA), 1990, p 141.
7. Jacques Derrida, *Specters of Marx: The State of the Debt, the Work of Mourning and the New International*, tr Peggy Kamuf, Routledge (Abingdon-on-Thames), 1994.
8. Ernst Cassirer, *An Essay on Man: An Introduction to a Philosophy of Human Culture*, Yale University Press (New York), 1944.
9. Jacques Derrida in *Ghost Dance*, directed by Ken McMullen, Channel 4 Television, 1983.

Daniel Libeskind, 'The Head', *Theatrum Mundi*, 1985

Hovering just beyond our perceptual reach and sensory grasp, the dynamic forces and communicative agencies that haunt Libeskind's imagined city, Theatrum Mundi, are intangible and insubstantial, yet they have a profound impact on the material world they invade and pervade. As our world becomes ever more insubstantial, we must find a way to navigate these new and emergent conditions; we must rekindle architecture's long romance with the ghost.

Text © 2024 John Wiley & Sons Ltd. Images: p 6 © Future Publishing Ltd; p 7 © Moviestore/Shutterstock; pp 8, 14 © Daniel Libeskind; p 9 © Mathew Emmett; pp 10–11 © Soyun Lim

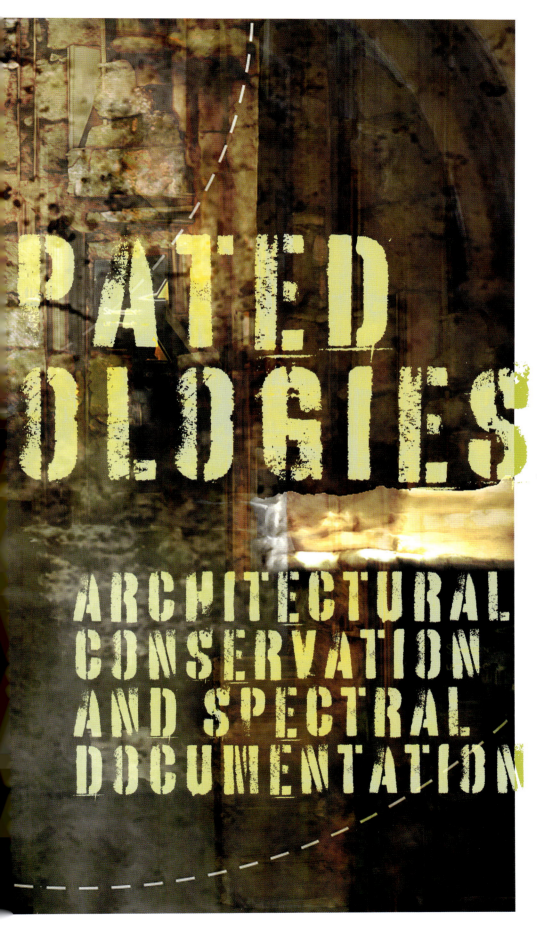

Cameron Stebbing

Cameron Stebbing,
Recording the Marks of Conservation (detail),
Rievaulx Abbey (founded 1132), near Helmsley,
North Yorkshire, England,
2023

FROM ITS VERY INCEPTION, ARCHITECTURAL PRESERVATION, AND THE SPECIALIST CONSERVATION PRACTICES THAT HAVE EVOLVED TO SUPPORT IT, HAVE OCCUPIED A SHIFTING TERRITORY OF CONSTANT QUANTIFICATION AND CONTINUALLY EVOLVING LEGISLATION.

Since the formalisation of architectural conservation as a discipline, beginning in the 19th century, the question of how to integrate and present built heritage within the landscape has evolved numerous strategies for the practical care and preservation of buildings. However, in a postmodern context emptied of the symbolic cosmological realms of the past and defined by technological mediations of the world, French philosopher Jean Baudrillard posits a strong nostalgic tendency for a vital relationship to the 'real' as symptomatic of a hyperreal social setting.[1] Historic places, from which such an authenticity can emanate, have also become classified and laid bare within a global heritage tourism industry.[2]

This proliferation of heritage is founded upon a proliferation truth; the expulsion of uncertainty and an exposition of authenticity through which buildings enter into the realm of heritage. A neutral and static definition of an object reveals why it must be preserved. But, as such places gain significance in relation to their histories, they evoke an additional temporal dimension from which a profound ambiguity emanates. Beyond this fixation of objects within technical and legal frameworks for the 'physical' care of buildings, there is an ontological uncertainty which haunts these clear renditions of heritage.

Proposed in his 1849 architectural treatise *The Seven Lamps of Architecture*,[3] Victorian cultural critic John Ruskin's 'golden stain of time' is analysed through themes developed in object-oriented ontology revealing syncopated temporal frames which blur the boundaries between the physically present and absent in architectural heritage. Such a reading situates historic architectural objects as sites which can be read beyond anthropocentric framings and incorporate questions not only of their preservation, but of their inevitable disappearance. The visual 'artefacts' illustrated here, constructed from experimental documentations taken from three 12th-century Cistercian abbeys in England (favoured subjects of Ruskin), shun their reification within specific mediums and reveal the incandescent flickering of multitudinous chronologies.

ARCHITECTURAL DESIGNER CAMERON STEBBING EVOKES A MENAGERIE OF PHILOSOPHICAL IDEAS USED TO ILLUSTRATE AND EXPLORE THE NOTION THAT TRADITIONAL RECORDING TECHNIQUES IGNORE HIDDEN AND VEILED PRESENCES WITHIN OUR BUILT ENVIRONMENT.

Uneasy Truths

Here, two aspects of historic places are under observation, initially appearing contradictory but later becoming somewhat interchangeable. In the first instance the historic built environment is intrinsically involved with time. Not only as observed by Austrian art critic Alois Riegl in relation to marks of age,[4] but also in the gradual evolution of a place in relation to people and events. Any historic place has a causal dimension through which it emerges as significant. Secondly, it involves authenticity and the search for truthful elements within its 'fabric'. Unique factors which can be understood through stable definitions, akin to the curation of objects within the museum.

In 1132, the establishment and development of Rievaulx Abbey, near Helmsley in North Yorkshire, England, and its subsequent fall to ruin following the Reformation five centuries later, is a narrative which can be classified. This authentic narrative and picturesque character are set values which drive the pilgrimage of tourists to the historic site. Ironically the state

Cameron Stebbing,
Cloister Reconstruction Reconstructed,
Rievaulx Abbey (founded 1132), near Helmsley,
North Yorkshire, England,
2023

opposite: The strange encompassment of authentic and staged fabric within the documentary eye. The real cloister is labelled at plinth level whilst the reconstructed arches above are delineated as a mere reconstruction.

Cameron Stebbing,
Recording and Representations,
Fountains Abbey (founded 1132), Ripon,
North Yorkshire, England,
2023

above: Photogrammetry, photography, drawing and textual description are all utilised to construct definitions of historic places. They aim to produce truthful renditions of their subjects, but do they also constitute their own particular authenticities which diverge from those subjects and one another?

Cameron Stebbing,
Recording the Marks of Conservation,
Rievaulx Abbey, near Helmsley,
North Yorkshire, England,
2023

left: Various marks and symbols litter historic spaces. Cautionary warnings, direction arrows and information boards constitute instructions for safe and proper navigation. Are these manifestations subsidiary to the historic structure, or do they become an inherent part of it?

of the ruins is fixed not only in conception but form too, with the skeletal arches carefully posed through the use of concealed reinforced-concrete columns.[5]

Any conservational intervention is predicated upon clear understandings of a place's authentic qualities – aspects which are important specifically to that place, as opposed to somewhere else.[6] These are descriptions of a fixed vision, static in comparison to the gradual evolution of the site itself. However, by mitigating the natural degradation of the ruins, the condition of conservation emerges as neither wholly part of nor totally distinct from its object. Are the characteristics developed in this process a simple description or active prescription for the object?

To take another example, when architect and theorist Jorge Otero-Pailos uses latex solution to peel back layers of stains and dirt from a historic façade, subsequently displaying this patina adjacent to its host,[7] his work occupies this ambiguous zone. Does the new artefact constitute a subsidiary representation of the object, or, with its authentic marks which delineate the passing of time, is it an inherent part of it? Discourses regarding the 'museumification' of heritage as a static backdrop against its vital evolutionary realm are common, but perhaps do not tell the whole story.

Uncertain Times

The idea of a static rendition of truth extracted from the natural temporal evolution of a place, then, is untenable. However, this may be less to do with the falsity of heritage, but, rather, that the deferring to a notion of rigid and certain truth is an anthropocentrically scaled device. It maintains historic places as monumental and enduring in comparison to the ephemeral lives which play out within them. Just as a place is 'known', those who inherit it are also perceived.

In their book *Hyperobjects* (2013), philosopher Timothy Morton sets out a conception of time not as a fixed entity but as an emergent property of objects themselves.[8] Things such as climate change are seen as massively distributed spatial and temporal entities, hyper-objects,[9] unfolding over geological periods, with the era coined the Anthropocene marking the realisation that human history also operates upon such vast scales. Where heritage may venerate the artistic merit of carvings at a ruined abbey from centuries ago, the fact that the limestone from which they are carved was formed over hundreds of millions of years is far stranger. Over this period the ruins and we ourselves, despite any conservational project, will be nothing more than the fossilised creatures which constitute the rock itself.

Cameron Stebbing,
Photogrammetry Study,
Fountains Abbey, Ripon,
North Yorkshire, England,
2023

Carved masonry exhibits marks of decay due to weather, traces from the tools of the mason who carved the stone and even the fossilised remains of dead creatures which formed the geology over hundreds of millions of years. The swift mark of the tool in comparison to the formation of stone constitute temporal utterances which are strangely and ontologically different.

THE LAMP OF MEMORY COULD EQUALLY BE SEEN AS A COMMENTARY ON HOW GOOD SOCIETIES SHOULD CARE FOR THEIR ARCHITECTURAL PAST

And these periods are not passive revelations, but actively tear into anthropocentric world views. Where policies aimed at mitigating climate change are defined over decades, its effects will continue to be traceable millennia from now. These events cannot be seen as static backdrops but ones which are unfolding over much greater periods of time, ones which do not scale neatly for humans. The slow decay of ruins over five centuries is rivalled in time by the discarding of disposable wrappers which litter their corners.

The Golden Stain(s) of Time
Ruskin articulates the relationship between architecture and age within the sixth chapter of *The Seven Lamps*, 'The Lamp of Memory',[10] proclaiming the value of patinas which express the 'golden stain of time'. The presence of dust and degradation mark the endurance of a structure in undisputable honesty. He even placed value on what had been lost to erosion, 'half an inch down',[11] creating an interplay between presence and absence. Thus, restorative practices were viewed with disdain as acts of destruction, falsifying the honesty of a structure; its ultimate sacrifice was even viewed as a better outcome.[12]

That Ruskin's theory still maintains the aforementioned anthropocentric framing is not disputed. The lamp of memory could equally be seen as a commentary on how good societies should care for their architectural past. However, Morton takes the principal of the golden stain further, commenting that it approaches something akin to an ontological redefinition of things, where they are no more, or less, than the causal sum of what has happened to them.[13] The notion that things are 'stained' in this way radically subsumes all acts of preservation as constituent of the object itself.

Take the pollutants sedimented within Otero-Pailos's latex sheets: they cannot so easily be 'cleaned' away. Understanding climate in the Anthropocene means there is no easy ontological 'away' to which these stains can be banished.[14] Soot-blackened façades become quasi-ethical slices of geological scale. Does the recognition of pollution as ontologically part of the heritage of places relate only to their own fragility, or to the fragility of all human fabric?

With this in mind, it may be more appropriate to pluralise Ruskin's initial proposition as it reveals not a single linear chronology but numerous syncopated 'stains'. Syncopated in respect that they rarely neatly align and are never wholly intelligible, as intelligibility itself constitutes just one mode of understanding an object. They are flickering superposed temporalities which haunt any singular mode of interpretation. Push the see-saw too far in one direction, as in the extension of a vast truth-seeking project, and other traces become exorcised.

Documenting the Ghosts
How can the process of recording architecture, usually undisputed in its role as truth-seeker, acknowledge these multitudinous stains? Its nominal position lies in the establishment of objective knowledge upon which a conservation or preservation act can be predicated. Photography, for example, establishes objectivity in a documentary process, indisputably recording something at a particular moment in time. However, when advocating its early usage for recording façades, Ruskin urged a sensually close capture of the marks of age upon a building in a manner which is far more embodied than its current dissociated position.[15]

Similarly, by suspending nominal practice, the medium of photogrammetry, often used to record buildings, can admit traces of other temporal scales. Its usual use requires an object be recorded under certain conditions to collect the most accurate set of data. Overcast lighting ensures a good representation of materiality is captured, and point-cloud data – created from the comparison of similar photographs when constructing photogrammetric models – are meticulously cleaned to allow the representation to emerge clearly. By mitigating the process, one is actively promoting the maintenance of that single anthropocentric framework where objects are rendered transparently and emphatically.

Cameron Stebbing,
Pollution and Dust,
Kirkstall Abbey (founded 1152), Leeds,
West Yorkshire, England,
2023
The 19th-century cultural critic John Ruskin placed value in the accumulated marks of age on structures. Kirkstall Abbey's façade is stained and degraded with marks of pollution from its gradual evolution. Such stains not only record the structure's fragility but are a small utterance of the Anthropocene, a mark of a structure not within a nebulous environment, but a distinct fraction of it.

Cameron Stebbing,
Environmental Stains,
Rievaulx Abbey, near Helmsley,
North Yorkshire, England,
2023
The photogrammetric process captures more than just its intended subject. Traces of the environmental conditions become sedimented within reproduced digital models. Here, climate conditions are translated as surface conditions, constituting a single object.

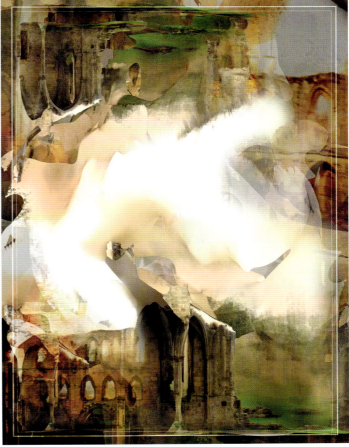

Cameron Stebbing,
Occupation versus Documentation,
Rievaulx Abbey, near Helmsley,
North Yorkshire, England,
2023

opposite: Ruskin's call for amateur photographers to closely document façades without recourse to proper perspectival composition are echoed in the manifestations of time, position and experience subsumed within the photogrammetry reconstructions. Such unwanted signatures, usually expelled from proper documentary representations, are here juxtaposed and mapped, constructing the view and speed of the recorder as an inherent part of the artefact itself.

Cameron Stebbing,
Shrine and Piscina,
Rievaulx Abbey, near Helmsley,
North Yorkshire, England,
2023

left: At one point these two elements were central to the daily religious rituals which took place at the abbeys. Today the purposeful procession of monks is replaced by the obsessive consumption of tourism.

Various strategies were used by the visual artefacts to draw out the ambiguity of the documentary process. By collecting data in harsh lighting conditions, effects of the environment are baked onto the surface of the reconstructed models themselves, translating the unique temporal signature of the recording as a small slice of the climate itself. The sky and clouds become obtrusively conflated with architectural form, whilst patinate stains seem to ripple over the surface of the images. They can no longer be seen as distinct from the environment within which they were constituted.

Furthermore, the re-inscription of the recorder themself is implied by the distorted views of the object. Akin to the prolonged exposure required by old photographs, the period within which the data was collected, as well as the specific position and sightlines of the observer, are sedimented into the reconstructions as stretched parallax effects and areas of absence.

The strangeness and uncertainty of the artefacts accounts for their unwillingness to make any one interpretation reign supreme. The marks of pollution evoke ethical responsibilities to climate, whilst the optical distortions fail to exorcise the highly personal and unobjective relationship between an occupant and building. Far from lamps which light the way, these cartographies record the shadowy illumination of mysterious chronologies.

Where nominal relationships with heritage require the documentation of present fabric, the elucidation of geological periods inscribes a radical and uncertain disappearance. In this reading, places of heritage are not passed down to known posterity, but ask potent questions of the fragility of who may be around to see them.

Did the builders of these places ever stop to think it would be their ruins we would venerate? 🗲

Notes
1. Jean Baudrillard, *Simulacra and Simulation*, University of Michigan Press (Ann Arbor, MI), 1994, p 6.
2. See Thordis Arrhenius, *The Fragile Monument*, Artifice (London), 2012, p 4.
3. John Ruskin, *The Seven Lamps of Architecture*, Dover (New York), 1989, p 187.
4. Alois Riegl, 'The Modern Cult of Monuments: Its Character and Origin', tr Kurt W Forster and Diane Ghirardo, in *Oppositions, 25*, Rizzoli (New York), 1982, pp 21–51.
5. See Peter Fergusson *et al*, *Rievaulx Abbey*, English Heritage (London), 2006, p 47.
6. See Paul Drury and Anna McPherson, *Conservation Principles, Policies and Guidance: For the Sustainable Management of the Historic Environment*, Liverpool University Press (Liverpool), 2008, p 22.
7. See Jorge Otero-Pailos, 'The Ethics of Dust' series: www.oteropailos.com/the-ethics-of-dust-series.
8. Timothy Morton, *Hyperobjects: Philosophy and Ecology after the End of the World*, University of Minnesota Press (Minneapolis, MN), 2013, pp 61–4.
9. *Ibid*, p 1.
10. Ruskin, *op cit*, pp 176–98.
11. *Ibid*, pp 194–5.
12. *Ibid*, p 196.
13. Timothy Morton, *All Art is Ecological*, Penguin Classics (London), 2018, p 90.
14. See Morton, *op cit*, p 31.
15. See Arrhenius, *op cit*, pp 77–84.

Text © 2024 John Wiley & Sons Ltd. Images © Cameron Stebbing

Eva Menuhin

UNCERTAINTY

Captivate: Spatial Modelling Research Group
(Simon Withers and Steve Kennedy),
3D scans of St George's Garrison Church,
Greenwich, London,
2023
The church was designed by the brothers Thomas Henry and Matthew Digby Wyatt and built between 1862 and 1863. This 3D digital section is of the apse – its structure, mosaics and surrounding trees. Multilayered and complex 3D scans such as these are made using light waves (LiDAR) but scans can also be made using radio waves (radar) and sound waves (sonar). Such remote-sensing technologies are used to make digital shadows of things in the physical world without damaging or touching them. Photography and drawing are also forms of remote sensing.

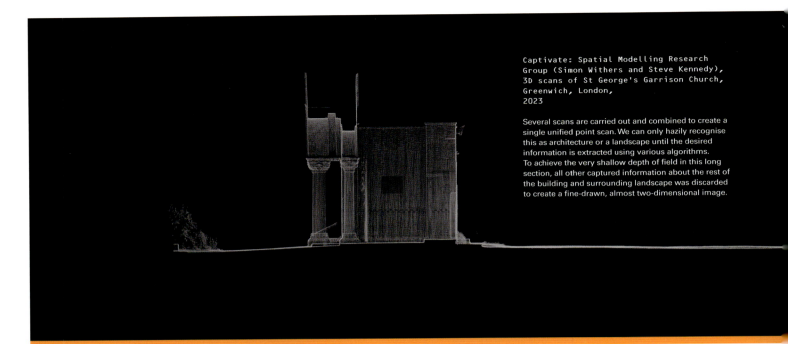

Captivate: Spatial Modelling Research Group (Simon Withers and Steve Kennedy), 3D scans of St George's Garrison Church, Greenwich, London, 2023

Several scans are carried out and combined to create a single unified point scan. We can only hazily recognise this as architecture or a landscape until the desired information is extracted using various algorithms. To achieve the very shallow depth of field in this long section, all other captured information about the rest of the building and surrounding landscape was discarded to create a fine-drawn, almost two-dimensional image.

LAID BARE BY CONTEMPORARY SCANNING TECHNIQUES AND TECHNOLOGIES, HISTORIC BUILDINGS REVEAL A SERIES OF NESTED, DIAPHANOUS PRESENCES – THE MEMBRANES OF MEMORY AND FRAGMENTS OF HISTORY. ARCHITECTURAL WRITER EVA MENUHIN INVESTIGATES A RECENT PROJECT BY THE UNIVERSITY OF GREENWICH'S CAPTIVATE: SPATIAL MODELLING RESEARCH GROUP, WHOSE GOSSAMER-THREADED ARCHITECTURAL REPRESENTATIONS DECODE TIME, MOVEMENTS, CHANGES, ADDITIONS AND DESTRUCTIONS OF A LONDON GARRISON CHURCH – A POETIC, GHOSTLY BALLET BETWEEN TIME, BUILDING AND NATURE.

Even viewed out of context, Captivate's 3D scans of the ruined St George's Garrison Church in Woolwich, in the Royal Borough of Greenwich in Southeast London, are aesthetically exquisite. Ghostly, delicate, evanescent, they are evocative of cobwebs, or the bloom of frost patterns on glass. They also have an innate quality that teases the analytical part of the mind and invites closer inspection.

Captivate: Spatial Modelling Research Group is based at the University of Greenwich. The group uses remote-sensing technologies – light detection and ranging (LiDAR) scanning, photogrammetry, ground-penetrating radar, hyper-spectral frequencies and drone surveys – to create 3D digital models that unite the elements of cultural landscapes and architectural heritage both above and below ground. At the Garrison Church, Captivate used simultaneous locating and mapping (SLAM) scanners. These devices use LiDAR to emit a series of laser light pulses at objects. By determining the time it takes for the signals to bounce off the objects and return to the sensor, they measure the distance from the device to the target object while keeping track of the device's location within the surrounding space being scanned. The resulting discrete data points create a 3D 'map' of the architecture's or landscape's spatial relationships and features.

Construction and Destruction
The Garrison Church was built between 1862 and 1863 on the orders of Lord Sidney Herbert, Secretary of State for War, to serve the Royal Artillery's officers and men. Facing the Royal Artillery Barracks in Woolwich (James Wyatt, 1806), it was designed by brothers Thomas Henry and Matthew Digby Wyatt in an Italian Romanesque style, patterned in the polychromatic brick typical of High Victorian architecture, with interior decoration influenced by the architectural and artistic Byzantine Revival of the mid-1800s. Between 1902 and 1903 enamel mosaic decorations were added to beautify the interior. These were manufactured in Antonio Salviati's famous workshops in Murano, Italy, in the style of the famous Byzantine mosaics from the Italian town of Ravenna, the seat of the Western Roman Empire in the 5th century BC. The church's surviving mosaics depict ancient Christian symbols such as the phoenix and peacock on panels between the chancel arches, birds perching in grape- and passion-flower vines on the spandrel panels, and the Sacred Lamb of God on a lunette.

An enamel mosaic panel of St George and the Dragon on a gold ground in the apse above the altar also survives intact. It was added between 1919 and 1920 as part of a memorial proposed in the Second World War to honour members of the Royal Artillery who had been awarded the Victoria Cross – Britain's highest military decoration. Their names are inscribed on marble panels above and to either side, joining memorials in other parts of the church to those who had fallen in previous wars. Two more recent bronze plaques memorialise eleven Woolwich men who died in service or by acts of terrorism since the Second World War.

On 3 July 1944, a German V1 bomb, one of Hitler's infamous 'doodlebugs', intended to terrify the citizens of London, destroyed the soaring roof and nave, and the subsequent fire burnt out the interior. Although a temporary roof was erected, aside from occasional services held in the gutted shell of the building, the church fell into disuse and neglect. In the 1950s it was cleared of rubble, but a rebuilding scheme came to nothing. The structurally unstable upper levels of the church were demolished in 1970, leaving the lower remnants to enclose a memorial garden laid out in the nave and aisles, and a cheap protective corrugated-iron roof was erected over the remains of the apse and altar. Only in 2011, more than 60 years after it had been destroyed, were the first serious steps taken to restore the site.

Ambivalent Time and Meanings
Churches exist on multiple planes of being, with overlapping meanings. As material articulations of faith, they encompass the expression of personal belief and communal worship in the present while linking to the architectural, religious and symbolic past; they are simultaneously mythic and real. In a sense they are places out of time with porous boundaries between matter and mind, the body and the spirit.

But what is the ruin of a church? And what to do with a ruined church? And who decides?

The selective process of remembrance is implicit in these questions, as is the inherent difficulty that ruins are subject to perpetual reinterpretation as new information is revealed and human narratives evolve. Ruins are structures whose spatiotemporal location is peculiarly dynamic; they exist in the present but evoke the past in our imaginations, are spaces within which presence and disappearance coexist. Moreover, although we invest all physical objects and structures with meaning, in terms of narrative church ruins (and mosque and temple ruins) are unlike others because of their already complex metaphysical significance.

This multidimensional fluidity is as characteristic of the digital model or ghost of a church as of the original. An individual scan is formed of millions of individual measurements, captured using multiple scans. The data accumulates into vast point clouds, galaxies of billions of points, universally though unevenly distributed as points of data. However, these are meaningless until various algorithms subsequently applied to the point clouds extract 3D data from the scans, separating the 'noise' of redundant data from the 'message' to create the desired X-ray-style images of a building or landscape. The process is analogous to the way our brain selectively interprets the photons of light emitted from or reflected off the physical objects around us to create the world we see. In both instances, our interpretation is integral to the result, which changes as our – or the algorithms' – point of focus alters or the meaning of the image shifts as information is reinterpreted.

Using these digital tools and methodologies to investigate and map buildings and landscapes enables kinds of perception that allow us to interact with the material world in completely novel ways, as the new technologies weave together the permanent and the transitory in time and space. In this context it is worth citing the Catholic cathedral of Notre-Dame (1163–1250), on the Île de la Cité in Paris, France, which was severely damaged during a structural fire in 2019. The work of the art historian Andrew Tallon, of Vassar College in Poughkeepsie, New York, has been indispensable to the process of restoring it to be true to the original in appearance, materials and construction techniques. Tallon began using laser scanners in 2010 to create immaculately accurate 3D models of Notre-Dame based on point clouds. He found that the forces of the arches, vaults, wind and weather had shifted the structure over time. Tallon said: 'Every building moves, it heaves itself out of shape when foundations move, when the sun heats up on one side.

How the building moves reveals its original design and the choices that the master builder had to make when construction didn't go as planned.'[1]

Because 3D LiDAR scanning is so precise, it can measure these movements to within an accuracy of several millimetres, looking deep into the past to capture the existing building in its true, imperfect dimensions in the present. According to Philippe Villeneuve, Architect-in-Chief of Historic Monuments in charge of Notre-Dame: '[Tallon's] scan enabled us to reconstruct the vaults without any hesitation from a dimensional or formal standpoint, and it also granted us total freedom to understand how [the cathedral] was made, to be able to rebuild it in a thoughtful, intellectual, and intelligent way.'[2]

Curated Ruins

In the immediate aftermath of the Second World War, a group of influential figures including architect Hugh Casson, TS Eliot, the director of the National Gallery Kenneth Clark and the economist John Maynard Keynes published a small pamphlet of essays in which they argued that some war-damaged London churches, especially those of particular architectural merit, ought to be preserved as ruins; memorials of war's destructiveness.[3] These ruins were to be carefully curated as memorial gardens that nevertheless embodied the devastation most of the country was busy trying to forget in the postwar frenzy of rebuilding its shattered infrastructure. Very few of these still exist. Most have been replaced with simple plaques or monuments, or, frequently, have been redeveloped. Real estate in London is valuable.

The Garrison Church was not especially old as churches go and was built on no ancient sacred site of worship. Its beauty lies only in its damaged mosaics. Its congregation shrank as the garrison diminished in size and importance over the 20th century and the Royal Artillery moved to the Salisbury Plain, more suited to modern live-firing exercises. And yet, seemingly against the odds, the Garrison Church has not only survived, retaining its original function as a place of worship, but has undergone a renaissance.

Stability in Transience

With the sky above and incomplete walls surrounding it, the open nave of the church is a familiar kind of space which is yet unfamiliar. What would ordinarily be a stone floor is grass; the former interior walls are warmed by the sun; rain, ice, clinging vines and animals are agents of transition. The stone and plasterwork reflect the

Captivate: Spatial Modelling Research Group (Simon Withers and Steve Kennedy), 3D scans of St George's Garrison Church, Greenwich, London, 2023

opposite: Each point is defined by its own XYZ coordinate position, typically rendered as a pixel, and point clouds are a collection of unique survey coordinates. By combining many scans, an accurate 3D model of an object can be described in a series of planes in space. This image shows a short section of the internal spaces of the entire church in multiple planes.

below: This planar short cross-section highlights the pulpit, on the right of the image, and the truncated pillars and their capitals that once supported the arch in front of the transept and apse. However precise the original scans are, because the data are a series of floating dots, the planes and edges seen in such a cross-section are the result of choices subject to permissible deviation according to algorithms which vary between kinds of software.

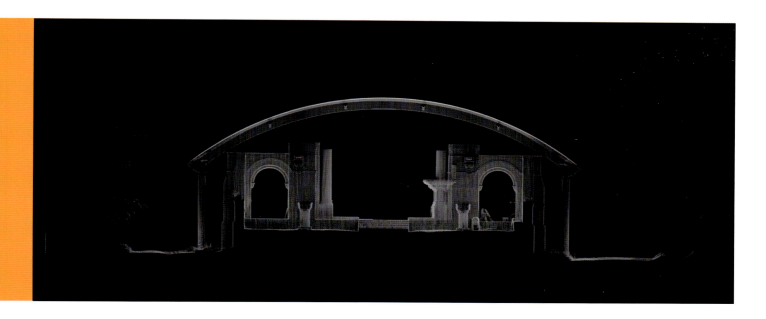

Captivate: Spatial Modelling Research Group (Simon Withers and Steve Kennedy), 3D scans of St George's Garrison Church, Greenwich, London, 2023

top: This deep scan shows how the church is embedded in the slightly slanting plot, with the crypt on the left, under the nave. The information will be useful during renovation of the crypt and eventually when building a Commonwealth and Gurkha Memorial Garden on the land northeast of the church. The uncertain quality of the edges and vegetation renders the image uncertain, smoke-like.

centre: The digital model of the church has many onion-like layers. Although the original digital data model is spatially highly accurate, the layers and interpretations of the data have evocative qualities. Here the remains of the vestibule, including the new gate, are depicted in a series of veils and shivering, uncertain textures.

bottom: While similar to a typical architectural plan view, a 3D scan such as this has a greater depth and an organic quality which is more reminiscent of a transparent organism under a microscope than a piece of architecture.

structure's vicissitudes over time. The beauty here is that of the imperfect and transient, the ever-renewing and changing. It is also a place of stories, such as those of the men whose memory is quietly celebrated here, of a devastated church reincarnated as a place of peace, and an invitation to recognise the possibility of fluidity in what we often regard as static.

In 2011, Heritage Lottery Fund grants made it possible to stabilise the structure and erect a graceful tensile fabric roof to protect the mosaics, apse, pulpit and altar while creating a covered stage for services and other events. In 2015 there was a further grant from the Heritage fund and also from Historic England (then English Heritage) to support additional restoration works. In 2018 the management of the church was taken over by the Woolwich Garrison Church Trust. New wrought-iron security gates, designed by Peter Preston of Manifest Design Workshop, Oxford, were inaugurated that same year. Painted blue, as they would have been in Victorian times, the design incorporates the Crimea cannon from the Royal Artillery cap badge and the flags and drums associated with the regiment. Intertwined stems of the flowers of remembrance – the poppy (UK), the cornflower (France) and the forget-me-not (Germany) – form the gate's vertical elements. Gilded birds represent the lark, evoking the famous verse in John McCrae's 1915 poem *In Flanders Fields*:

> In Flanders fields the poppies blow,
> Between the crosses, row on row,
> That mark out place; and in the sky
> The larks still bravely singing fly
> Scarce heard amid the guns below.[4]

Transparency is often equated with truth. LiDAR scans invite us to peer deep into the structures of a building and the closer we look, the greater the temptation to think we understand it fully as its secrets are revealed. Yet, while their almost uncanny precision can make it possible to see not only the hidden reality but reveal the past, there is an inherent contradiction in this confident association of data and truth. Analogous to the way a painting disintegrates into meaningless patches of colour when we get too close, we need to pull back to comprehend the whole.

Because digital models embrace the margins of data, ambiguity and invention, the church's digital twin is more like a crystal ball than a model. Visions dissolve and resolve into ghostly forms, shifting veils and parallel worlds, depending on the point of view. The scans might almost be depicting the spiritual presence of the church, the idea of it, an invisible, underlying structure that has grown out of an emotional relationship between people, place and faith which has given the church its resilience.

On Remembrance Sunday the wrought-iron gates open onto the garden. Grapevines cling to the low remnants of the surrounding walls and the scent of late blossoms and damp leaves fills the air. Representatives from the local community are there, from the Armed Forces and Army Cadets, and members of the local Gurkha community, as are soldiers from the barracks and their families. There is a service. The ever-shifting point cloud of individual memories, faiths, histories and hope – like a murmuration of starlings – coalesces and settles for an hour or few in a garden.[5] ⌂

Notes
1. Quoted in Rachel Hartigan, 'Historian Uses Lasers to Unlock Mysteries of Gothic Cathedrals', *National Geographic*, 16 April 2019: www.nationalgeographic.com/adventure/article/150622-andrew-tallon-notre-dame-cathedral-laser-scan-art-history-medieval-gothic.
2. Quoted in Lindsay Cook, 'Leaving a Trace', Vassar College, Poughkeepsie, New York, 16 November 2023: www.vassar.edu/news/leaving-a-trace.
3. Hugh Casson *et al*, *Bombed Churches as War Memorials*, The Architectural Press (London), 1945.
4. John McCrae, 'In Flanders Fields', first published in *PUNCH*, 8 December 1915, p 468.
5. With grateful thanks to Tim Barnes MBE KC, Chairman of the Woolwich Garrison Church Trust, for his invaluable time and assistance.

Text © 2024 John Wiley & Sons Ltd. Images © Simon Withers and Steve Kennedy

Haunted Houses

Architecture and Large Language Models

Chris Speed

Considering the vast datasets that constitute artificial intelligence, it might be assumed that there is no place for the ghostly or ambiguous among the binary logics of the all-knowing algorithm. Explaining that this is not in fact the case, Melbourne-based Professor of Design for Regenerative Futures **Chris Speed** reveals the tumult of numinous spirits that haunt the data, influencing and impacting the resultant texts and images.

Medieval etchings and scratchings in the floor of the Masons' Loft, York Minster, England, photographed 2022
Detailed study of the tracing-floor of the Masons' Loft reveals information about the construction of the cathedral – a topography of marks, scratches and 'pin' holes that were used to plot out elements of its design. Simultaneously it documents a condition of erasure in which new layers of gypsum are poured onto the floor to erase previous datasets.

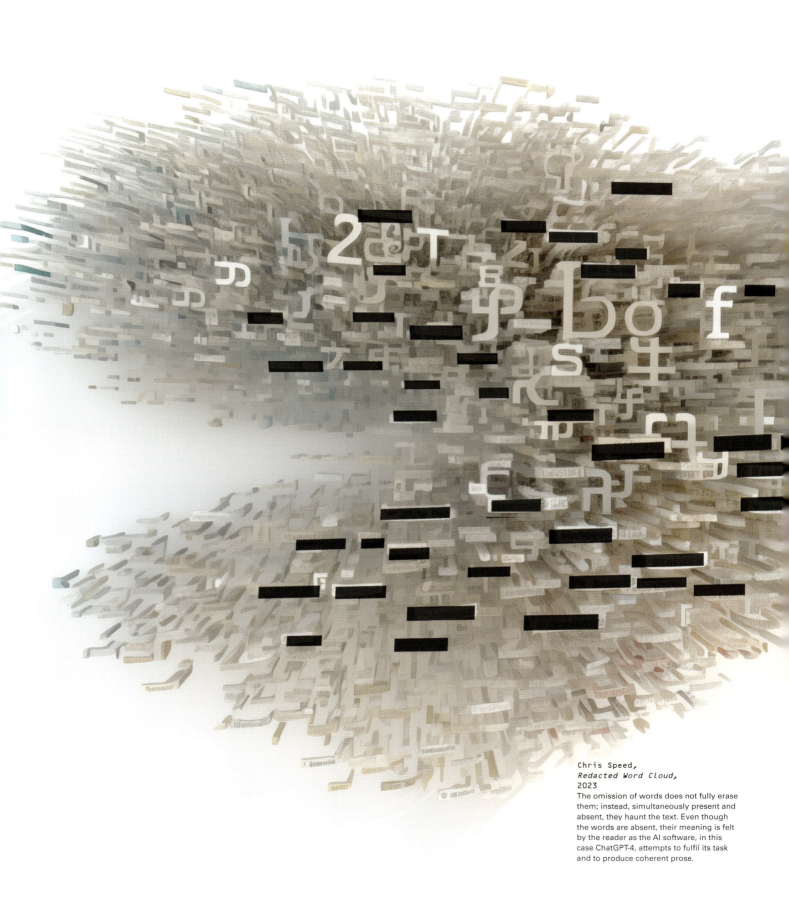

Chris Speed,
Redacted Word Cloud,
2023
The omission of words does not fully erase them; instead, simultaneously present and absent, they haunt the text. Even though the words are absent, their meaning is felt by the reader as the AI software, in this case ChatGPT-4, attempts to fulfil its task and to produce coherent prose.

Contractors' notes, comments and instructions on a construction site in Edinburgh, Scotland, photographed 2023
The act of inscribing of information about construction onto the building is hardly redundant; any visit to a contemporary construction site will reveal a wealth of contractors' notes, markups and instructions. These datasets are rarely erased and often become covered, painted over or simply buried by subsequent layers of materials.

The way of the ghost is haunting, and haunting is a very particular way of knowing what has happened or is happening. Being haunted draws us affectively, sometimes against our will and always a bit magically, into the structure of feeling of a reality we come to experience, not as cold knowledge, but as a transformative recognition.
— Avery Gordon, *Ghostly Matters: Haunting and the Sociological Imagination*, 1996[1]

When AI systems replicate and expose, as they so often do, the powerful patterns of human exclusion, discrimination and cruelty embedded in our own data, we are not seeing a machine spontaneously form racist or sexist or ableist intentions. We are seeing electronic ghosts of our own injustice and cruelty, reanimated in software … We are not being oppressed by a new, inhuman mechanical evil. We are being haunted by our own ghosts.
— Shannon Vallor, 'Artificial Intelligence and Humanity's Future: A Ghost Story', 2023[2]

First published in 1996, Avery Gordon's *Ghostly Matters* conceptualised ghosts and hauntings as a means of sensitising the sociologist to events, experiences or affects that do not conform to the model of the everyday. Yet, whilst we have barely seen three full decades pass since then, Shannon Vallor's short essay 'Artificial Intelligence and Humanity's Future (2023) explores a radically changed sociocultural and technological landscape, acknowledging the troubled nature of the datasets that produce what we naively/reductively describe as AI. Loaded with bias, discrimination and privilege, these datasets are haunted by our historical prejudices, and those using them are likely to perpetuate this cycle. The history and future of architectural design has always been weighed down with a combination of images that guide young designers towards 'what buildings should look like', and regulatory guidelines that steer architects towards predefined 'safe' outputs. Between the worlds that Gordon and Vallor describe in the quotes here, we are reminded of the ghosts that haunt architecture.

Representational Cultures
The societies we experienced in 1996 and 2023 seem literally worlds apart, distanced by the single, most profound development in many of our lives – the internet, and all of the corresponding services of the digital economy. Nevertheless, Gordon's and Vallor's narratives share a deep sensibility that warns us of the determined nature of particular representational cultures, the belief that the abstraction of the world enables us to measure, explain and, in turn, organise complex phenomena. In between, every aspect of society has become underpinned by data-driven systems rooted in Newtonian and Cartesian principles to abstract the world. Dan McQuillan explains the way in which machine learning manipulates data points – ranging from tumour scans to literary works – to conform to mathematical models.[3] This process is manifested in activation functions, algebraic elements driving input-output mapping in neural network nodes, but despite their pervasive use in decision-making across various sectors, algorithms never attain a meaningful understanding of complex social situations or literature. Instead, they become proficient at categorising data to make mathematical (representational) based decisions.

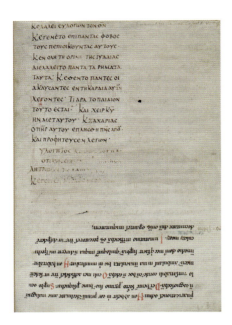

Page from *Codex Sangallensis 18* (9th century) at the Abbey Library of Saint Gall in St Gallen, Switzerland, photographed 2020

The lower text belongs to the Gospel of Luke in Greek, and the upper text is Latin Vulgate. The erasure and deliberate occlusion of words and the shifting of syntax, language and meaning is not a new phenomenon nor is it exclusive to AI or digital media. For centuries, the practice of writing on wax tablets and velum meant any act of authorship was accompanied by an act of erasure – the deletion of an earlier text – to make way for new writings. Not unlike the ChatGPT prompt, however, these subsequent reworkings of the page obeyed certain rules to promote legibility and understanding.

In architectural design, the distance between the past and the present has been closing for a long time. The tracing-floors within the Masons' Loft at York Minster (constructed between 1230 and 1472) reveal a bridge between the representational modes, where the plans for the cathedral, originally drawn on velum, are translated into 'life-sized' projections marked out with pins and rope on the gypsum drafting floor. In turn these 'one to one' diagrams became the basis for templates and patterns, made of wood or lead, that the masons used to mark out the stone prior to cutting and carving, the syntax of drafting becoming embedded in the structure of the building. To this day contractors continue to scribble their interpretations of plans and instructions for colleagues, and write and draw inappropriate jokes on the plasterboard of building sites before they are lost to plaster and paint, the database of the site becomes an intrinsic part of the completed building.[4]

Suppressing the Ghosts

Curious about how we might reveal some ghostly behaviour, and to underscore the representational construction of language that allows common AI tools to appear coherent, the Story Exhaustion Generator[5] was developed in conjunction with digital education specialist Javier Tejera to see if we could, as Gordon has put it, begin 'meddling with taken-for-granted realities'.[6] But first let us explain in simple terms how words are associated in such a way as to generate meaningful statements. The corpus of text that exists within a large language model such as GPT-3 or GPT-4 will have been broken into words that become known as tokens. Each token is represented as a high-dimensional vector, which captures the semantic meaning of the token. The model will have been trained on vast amounts of text data to learn these embeddings, inspired by linguist John Rupert Firth's eloquent principle that 'you shall know a word by the company it keeps'.[7] This allows any output of the model to reflect the probability distribution over the vocabulary, and in turn predicts the likelihood of each token in the vocabulary being the next token in the sequence. Interestingly, as the text is generated the model can either sample from the predicted distribution to choose the next token randomly, or it can choose the token with the highest probability, which is known as 'greedy decoding'.

Given the determination with which tools such as ChatGPT seek to generate outputs that correspond with the expectations of the human, it seemed a playful conceit to force it to not repeat words that were core to the meaning of the text, by utilising the ChatGPT-4 prompt: *'In the following text I want you to take any word which is used more than once and replace all uses of it after the first one with an alternative word or phrase that contains the same meaning. Ignore structural words like "a", "the" etc.'*

The use of the ghost as a metaphorical model to contest the determinism and to reveal an uncanniness is perhaps the most obvious bridge between Gordon's and Vallor's work.

The illustrations here demonstrate the tenacity of rules and models, highlighting the tendency of representational models of language to be guided by underlying syntactical structures that inevitably haunt any system. As data-driven technologies continue to regulate architectural design and construction, we can already imagine the 'large architectural models' that will pre-empt the next generation of drawings and buildings. From the regulatory guidelines that steer designers towards placing doors, windows and stairs in appropriate and safe combination with one another, repeating a history of assumptions about people, environment and cultures, to the next generation of architecture students who borrow the same books from the library that perpetuate images of what architecture should be and what it can be – architecture's dataset is as haunted as any house that we will find. ⌂

Notes
1. Avery Gordon, *Ghostly Matters: Haunting and the Sociological Imagination*, University of Minnesota Press (Minneapolis, MN), 1997, p 8.
2. Shannon Vallor, 'Artificial Intelligence and Humanity's Future: A Ghost Story', The New Reel, 13 October 2023: www.newreal.cc/magazine/a-ghost-story.
3. Dan McQuillan, 'Data Science as Machinic Neoplatonism', *Philosophy & Technology* 31(2), 2017, pp 253–72.
4. Dermott McMeel, Richard Coyne and John Lee, 'Talking Dirty: Formal and Informal Communication in Construction Projects', in Bob Martens and André Brown (eds), *Computer Aided Architectural Design Futures 2005: Learning from the Past*, Springer (Vienna), 2005, pp 265–74.
5. https://ai-labs.efi.ed.ac.uk/storyexhaustion.
6. Gordon, *op cit*.
7. John Rupert Firth, *Studies in Linguistic Analysis*, Wiley-Blackwell (Oxford), 1957, p 11.
8. Vallor, *op cit*.

Text © 2024 John Wiley & Sons Ltd. Images: pp 34–5 © Photographer Peter J Baldwin. Reproduced with the kind permission of the York Chapter; pp 36–7, 39 © Chris Speed. AI-generated images created in Midjourney; p 37(t) © Ingrid Heersche

Chris Speed,
Reconstructing Le Corbusier using language prompts to explore space grammars,
2023

The notion of latent languages and ghostly grammars within architecture naturally begets the question of the haunting presences of architectures absent and unbuilt. Like many of his contemporaries and forebears, Le Corbusier posited a set of rules or principles for the design of architecture. Using Midjourney, and the prompt 'using Le Corbusier's 5 points of architecture to generate missing designs', it has been possible to develop a series of building designs that conform to Le Corbusier's syntactic structure, bringing the ghosts of unfulfilled architectural potential to life.

architecture's dataset is as haunted as any house that we will find

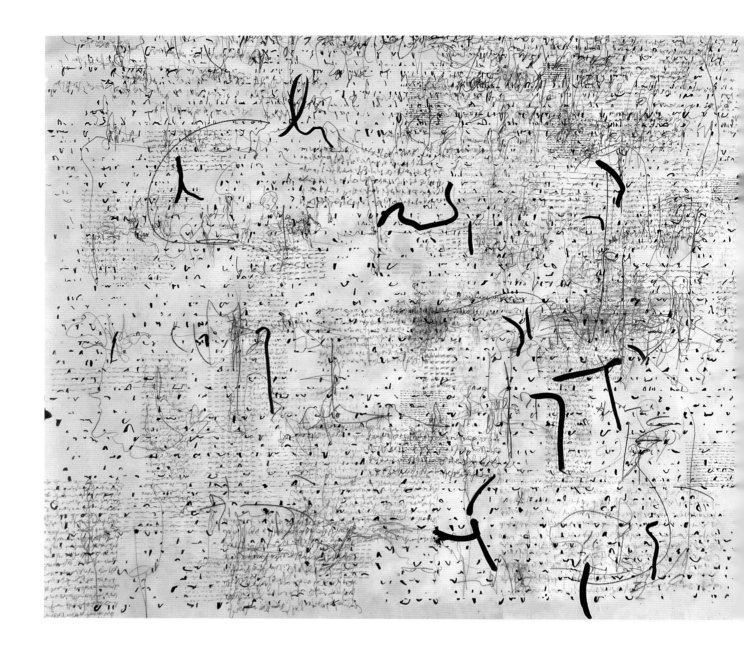

Generations of contradicting human rule have rendered the forest indecipherable. Each leader, landowner, laird, lender, draws out their plan with graphs and tallies, claims and convictions. Each defies, ignores the last. Fierce assertions of dominance, wartime desperations and defensive stands. Taking stock, keeping count, focused on their measure. Negotiations, stiff back-handers hidden from public eye, revelations and justifications. The value of value is radically thought, rethought, re-rethought. 4,000 acres for the price of 290. How much for a tree? It depends how straight it is. Conservation chimes in its active nothings and soft regret, frustrated attempts to make things right. 400,000-plus pines and counting, waiting, waiting, ripped out again. Caring or careful? A chasm exists between the two. Considered sacrifice made here for there. Acres disregarded, deemed too far gone. Carbon-offset plantations bear their breathing rates in orange, blue and

PHANTOMS OF A FIVE-DAY FOREST

Kirsty Badenoch

Strangely, the palimpsest of human occupation is often far less visible in the city than it is in wilder spaces. Artist, architect, researcher and educator **Kirsty Badenoch** describes an exploratory expedition to draw out these ghosts within the rugged landscapes of the Scottish Highlands, and a subsequent exhibition of the work through diary entries and photographic forms. The work itself is made through transcriptive collaborations with the volatile climate and flora and fauna of the site, creating a tale of palimpsestuous relationships that dislocate the artistic self as nature leads the dance, or at the very least calls the tune.

Kirsty Badenoch,
- - o o 0)) ..-- - -. . (Overwriting),
Northwest Highlands, Scotland,
April 2023
Centuries of written and rewritten rules have shaped and scarred the land. Though long defunct, each is evident through its haunting of today's ecological make-up.

purple. This type of felling is good, that is bad. Mass planting is a lethal act. Winching a soft form of birth. This land is haunted by so many forms of death.

I have travelled to the far northwest of the Scottish Highlands on the one bus per week that bumps east–west along 'Destitution Road', with writer Tom Jeffreys. Our destination, Beinn Eighe, is the UK's first state-owned and operated nature reserve, purchased in 1951. It comprises part of the boreal forest, or taiga – the world's largest and oldest forest ecosystem circling the breadth of the Northern Hemisphere, and dating back to the glacial retreat. In Scotland, only a few small remnants of old-growth forest remain, and they are largely in the possession of a few private landowners. This place bears testimony to some of the oldest and most pressing problems of how power and control have misshaped and continue to misshape our world. I am here to engage with a complex, scarred and cacophonous terrain. I am here to meet its ghosts.

A forest does not conform by the rules that denote a territory, it cannot be predicted, it does not abide by hard lines and hierarchies

Territory

The desire to assert order and control has for centuries ruled the Western attitude to land. Even the notion of territory is itself highly problematic. It is a political technology that cleaves, sections and assigns categorised portions to the jurisdiction of sovereign rule.[1] It reduces interconnected places to disembodied, quantifiable geophysical assets. It administers a value system based on an immediate present, and in doing so fails to acknowledge the value of embedded and embodied histories, species, habitats and geologies. Whether land management is driven by profit, war, conservation, eco-tourism or any other anthropocentric aim, the assetisation of the land establishes a fundamental oversimplification and illusion of control, notions that are deeply destructive.

The architectural profession has been founded on these same systems of power and control; systems set up to serve patriarchal, colonial and anthropocentric frameworks. The architectural process as set out in the RIBA Plan of Work is to strategise (stage 0), plan (stages 1–3), coordinate (stage 4), execute (stages 5–6) and abandon (stage 7).[2] A large part of this process requires prediction and projection. This fundamental belief that humans can predict has reinforced an illusion of control, and hence the domination over nature.[3]

A forest does not conform by the rules that denote a territory, it cannot be predicted, it does not abide by hard lines and hierarchies. Beings and bodies haunt one another – past generations of decayed creatures feed new growth, the mulch from trees a thousand years past is present in the soil of today. Lichens perfectly embody the relational ontology of the forest. Lichens are not themselves organisms, but exist as a stable symbiotic association between a specific type of fungus and algae. The self, or the form, exists as a practice of mutual interdependency.

As we creep slowly out of the Anthropocene, the term 'symbiocene' has been used to describe a

forthcoming era of harmonious thinking, social equity and interspecies collaboration.[4] The symbiocene encompasses contemporary relational movements such as environmental justice, civil rights, feminism, indigenous knowledge and multispecies ethnography. This world of interactions and exchanges will require a very different architect to that of anthropocentric plans and strategies. It will require connectedness and spirit to become our material foundation.

The symbiotic architect finds their compass is far too sharp, ruler too straight, Rhino model too precise. AI-generated imagery convinces better than they do, and their catchphrase hooks are naive and flimsy. What does the symbiotic architect look like, and how do they spend their time? Can our profession allow itself to be purposely vague, emotional, indecisive, even feral? Rather than makers of marks, can we allow ourselves to be the ones who are marked upon? Would we be prepared to relinquish our control?

The Five-Day Forest
For five days, the remnant of old-growth forest around Beinn Eighe becomes my drawing studio. I choose not to set up in the Nature Reserve idyll. Instead, each day I climb the fence and scale the ditch of a private plantation that runs astride Destitution Road. The occasional passing freight-truck projects thunderous echoes each time one crosses the cattle grid. The roar of a long-forgotten prehistoric beast, I jump out of my skin every time.

I stand. I listen. The forest is dark and dense and steep. Any former-deemed 'usefulness' long abandoned, no human has trodden here in years. The leaning hollowed trunks creak under their own decomposition. The mosses exhale damp clouds which cool and condense into streams. Ghostly whispers echo across epochs, far louder than any freight-truck could. I unroll my paper.

Kirsty Badenoch,
Five-day forest studio,
unnamed old-growth forest plantation,
Northwest Highlands,
Scotland,
April 2023
opposite: Former primordial forest, this land was cultivated into forestry plantation under private ownership. Now abandoned, its ghosts re-echo its 11,000-year-old origins.

Kirsty Badenoch,
Drawing imprint in moss,
unnamed old-growth forest plantation,
Northwest Highlands,
Scotland,
Wednesday 5 April 2023
left: The absence of a former drawing leaves its rectangular memory in the forest floor.

Kirsty Badenoch,
'Falling, Fallen, Felled',
unnamed old-growth forest plantation,
Northwest Highlands,
Scotland,
Thursday 6 April 2023
right: Sticks dropped in the overnight storm preserve areas of white, while pools collect and reflect the forest in their furrows.

Wednesday 5 April 2023
opposite: The battered paper skin is slung as a tent across its fallen ancestor, each holds up the other.

Tuesday / 05:00 / sunrise
This white square absence forms a perfect hole in the middle of the deer path. I sit for hours, maybe days, maybe weeks; my heartbeat slowing to match the pulse of the forest. I circle the square. I try to draw but my arms aren't long enough. My feet already sodden from the damp moss, this is a boundary I cannot cross. I can find no way in. It is too clean for this place, every intervention is rude, stark, simplistic. Ink falls with a futile thump. I stare into the white emptiness. Unbearably straight, clear, direct. It doesn't belong here, it is from another order. The deer avoid it, so do I. Inhospitable, inaccessible, I leave it there.

Tuesday / 10:00 / mist
I leave the studio to walk a line that doesn't exist. The ownership boundary between Nature Scot and the adjacent private landowner, who still refuses to sell. Navigating through orange-highlighter marked-up OS maps, the beginning is announced by a wooden road sign with aptly cut-out mountains and pines. Then nothing. To the left are spruce fields planted in the 1960s, to the right abandoned scrub and stumps for miles. At the summit, it is shockingly easy to trace the orange highlighter lines over the land. Those power lines have shaped it all. Only on the physical land, a line is not a single thin edge. The edge of deforestation bleeds deep into the forest, the negatives bare more impact than the positives. I knew this was the case on paper, but it was not until now that I really felt it.

Wednesday / 03:00 / storm
I am woken at night by howling rains. Nightmares about that pure white square. Will it endure? I didn't think it mattered but it seems that it does. I must have left a little part of myself out there in those hollow marks, a foreign body in a foreign place, shivering.

Wednesday / 08:45 / mist
I return to the studio. It is soaked, unrecognisable, amazing. Transformed into a topography of tiny rivulets and lochs in which the entire forest is reflected. A slug has dared explore, drawn a slimy path, eaten a corner. Fallen needles cast shadows and bleed sap. The paper has become its own terrain without me. I lift it from the floor, an impression of its form remains in the moss. A second hole created by the absence of the former. The imprint of a tent, of someone who slept here in the woods last night.

Wednesday / 17:00 / rain
I leave the papers hanging to dry: like great bed sheets strung out across fallen trunks, a moment of domesticity. But left out, the rain rains on, and the topography, the exchange, the creation and loss, dissolves into memory. Ink and Miracle-Gro slide off and soak back into the forest floor. The moss will grow slightly brighter here tomorrow. Dissolves also does the compacted square impression on the ground. Wet paper rips, a hole again, only slightly less white than before. Everything undone. I bring it home.

Thursday / 09:30 / more rain
I set up once more. This time we draw together, the rain and I in unison. We guide, extend, redraw one another's lines, suggesting springs and waterfalls, connecting rivers and lochs. Gold and midnight, iridescent and swirling. We are vibrant, fluid, alive. The drawing evolves second by second, I can't keep track. Hypnotic moments disappear, intensity fades and is replaced by new ridges and valleys and pools. Exchanges renegotiate. Something has shifted in the landing of sound. The ink and rain now beat together, rich with life.

Thursday / 19:00 / mist
My protective paper shelter has failed to fix the story. The ink has faded back once more, next to nothing remains. My skin becomes the territory of ticks and midges, they burrow and bite into me. Dissolved and disillusioned, I carry the worn white skin back down the road, a flag for the fallen down Destitution Road, broken in heavy arms.

Friday / 17:00 / dry
I sit for hours before moving. Wrapped up in itself long and thin, I rest my weight on it. The trunk of a gleaming white birch among birches. No longer quite white. I begin again. New ground, drawing water from the bog.

Saturday / 05:30 / sunrise
The battered skin emerges then falls back as light and colour fill the forest. An apparition maybe, no longer foreign. It is somehow of this place now. A blur. A skin, my skin, the skin of the forest. Its own skin. Hanging again as a tent, as the home I made here. Beaten, worn, the forest holds it up and it holds up the forest. I wrap it back around itself, a silver birch unpeeling.

Studio

Our hauntings complete, we head back to the city. The landscape becomes a territory once more, contained within its designated compartments. A 'favourite' place on a Google Maps list, a shelf of rolled-up papers, a funding report summary. And yet. The forest lingers, it haunts me back.

The process I undertook over those five days in the forest was beyond raw, it was deeply painful. At times I too dissolved with the ink – bodiless, vulnerable and quaking. There was terror in the surrender of my sense of solid self, my human agency and the marks that I make – my identity. There became a very different gauge of time, marked only by shifts in light and birdsong. I felt my whole internal system slow, become something other, bigger. Shedding my human skin allowed every growth and pain and whisper of the forest to flow right through me. In relinquishing myself, I become forest.

A few weeks later, I am introducing this year's design brief to a new class of second-year university students. As we pause for questions, one hand is raised. 'I sort of get that we don't have to design a building, but does our project need to be *useful*?'

Perhaps the most useful thing an architect can do is acknowledge that we cannot plan, we should not build and we have no agency to make decisions. Perhaps the most useful thing an architect can do is listen, gaze and surrender to our own ghostliness. Perhaps the most useful thing an architect can do is leave our papers out in the rain.[5]

Notes
1. Stuart Elden, 'Land, Terrain, Territory', *Progress in Human Geography* 34 (6), 2010, pp 799–817.
2. RIBA Plan of Work: www.architecture.com/knowledge-and-resources/resources-landing-page/riba-plan-of-work.
3. Caroline Merchant, *Reinventing Eden: The Fate of Nature in Western Culture*, Taylor & Francis/Routledge (New York), 2013, p 207.
4. Glenn A Albrecht, *Earth Emotions: New Worlds for a New World*, Cornell University Press (Ithaca, NY), 2019, p 102.
5. The work here is further documented in the collaborative artist book 'To an island on a loch, in an island on a loch', Mouldy Books, 2023 (available at https://tom-jeffreys.co.uk/product/to-an-island-in-a-loch-on-an-island-in-a-loch. With thanks to Tom Jeffreys, without whom this project would not be what it is.

Kirsty Badenoch,
'Falling, Fallen, Felled',
unnamed old-growth forest plantation,
Northwest Highlands, Scotland,
Saturday 8 April 2023
opposite: At dawn, this wavering blur haunts its own memory.

Kirsty Badenoch,
(), *Riverine* and *Chroma*,
'Falling / Fallen / Felled' exhibition,
Staffordshire St Gallery, Peckham,
London,
November 2023
above: Re-sited in the city, the drawings remember the manner in which they were made.

Text © 2024 John Wiley & Sons Ltd. Images: pp 40-46, © Kirsty Badenoch; p 47 © Kirsty Badenoch, photo Sheng Jung Ho

Designing Absence

The Invisible Bridge and the Ghost Barn

Ian Ritchie

River Itchen, South Downs National Park,
Twyford, Hampshire, England,
6 September 2021
The Invisible Bridge crosses one of the world's premier chalk streams, which along most of its length is designated a biological Site of Special Scientific Interest (SSSI) for its unique and rare ecology.

Straddling the fine line between architecture and art, London-based architects ritchie*studio have designed an Invisible Bridge and a Ghost Barn on a private, historic and protected estate in Hampshire, Southeast England. These delicate propositions juggle presence and absence informed by the site's history, by poetry, Charles Darwin, local flint and an intelligent and thoughtful client. **Ian Ritchie** writes about the concepts for these two interventions and their associated inspirational narratives.

Extant barn on the estate, Twyford,
Hampshire, England, 6 September 2021
The barn forms the east side of the former yard on
the estate. Barns are classic examples of vernacular
agricultural architecture, built using traditional carpentry
techniques requiring immense knowledge and skill.
No longer used for their original purposes, most such
buildings have become redundant, although their
multifunctional interior spaces make them suited to
contemporary and community uses.

A charter granted in the year 972 AD, during the reign of King Edgar, refers to an 'Egsanmor' (slaughter stone) in the village of Twyford, Hampshire. In the north part of Twyford is the 10.5-acre estate that is the site for two interventions designed by ritchie*studio: an Invisible Bridge crossing the River Itchen and the Ghost Barn. The location is within the South Downs National Park. It is classified as a Site of Special Scientific Interest and a Special Area of Conservation. The client studied biology, is a writer, was a sailor, and is engaged in resolving challenging business problems of international companies, the most significant one of which is based in Piedmont, Italy, which historians have described as having a centuries-old 'invisible bridge' with the UK.[1]

This background was an invisible aspect of the context of a potential project to renovate two 18th-century barns on the grounds of the estate. One was almost untouched, uninsulated, with a glorious interior of natural materials and an expressed structure of posts, tie beams, inclined queen-post trusses, wind bracing, purlins and rafters. One conclusion at the end of the inspection and discussion was to level the earth floor in order to accept interlocking tiles as a temporary surface for events. The discussion segued into a conversation while walking around the estate to better understand its history, folklore, topography and nature.

Charles Darwin took a daily walk along a triangular route called the Sandwalk on the grounds of Down House, his estate in Kent – his 'thinking path'. As he walked through shady woods, along a hedge-lined field, an orchard and vegetable garden, using the time for uninterrupted thought and observation, he would kick a pebble from a pile kept for the purpose with each turn, the difficulty of the problem he was trying to resolve marked by their number.

The client had walked this path and visited the 12 Marc Chagall stained-glass windows in All Saints' Church in Tudeley, Kent, nearby.

Out of Sight
Walking alongside the River Itchen, which runs through the estate, conversation about nature, the mind and the surreal, and a leap of faith, led to the idea of an invisible bridge to cross the river – a shallow, slow-moving chalk stream where it is difficult to see the brown trout and salmon below the water's surface. Knowledge and memory say that they are there, but the colour of the riverbed's pebbles and its rugosity, its water flow and reflections, are such that they remain invisible but to the well-trained eye.

The Invisible Bridge would be known only to the client, her family and friends. Perhaps, in such a less demanding planning context, permission would be unnecessary for a work of art, a sculpture, occasionally kinetic. It would be barely visible from outside the estate, and only then when the client deployed it to cross the river. The client's own thinking path would embrace the Invisible Bridge, and until the particular problem she was engaged in was resolved, she could drop a pebble to the riverbed each time she crossed.

In his poem *Bridge for the Living* (1975), Philip Larkin wrote:

And now this stride into our solitude,
A swallow-fall and rise of one plain line,
A giant step for ever to include
All our dear landscape in a new design.
… Always it is by bridges that we live.[2]

The riverbank is higher on the west – possibly kingfisher territory – and marshy opposite, with tall grasses whose stems are well-suited to the protected southern damselfly (*Coenagrion mercurial*).

ritchie*studio, Invisible Bridge,
South Downs National Park,
Twyford, Hampshire, England,
2023

below and opposite bottom: Drawing showing the rack-and-pinion system of the Invisible Bridge; parked, and cantilevered over the River Itchen. The design of this lightweight aluminium structure forms a single-sided 'deck' hovering two metres above the river surface. It also provides a place to sit, legs hanging free, to appreciate the beauty of the water, its reflections, and the natural flora an fauna of this rare chalk-stream habitat.

opposite top: From its almost invisible location – a sculptural element set within the riparian vegetation – the aluminium bridge cantilevers 22 metres (72 feet) on demand to span the river by means of a carefully balanced rack-and-pinion system manually operated by a large wheel.

Suzanne's Invisible Bridge

Slip, silver, river,
cross me, slowly,
watch the light
dance upon me.

Slide, stroll, river
cross me, happily,
let the air
caress my cheeks.

Time to ponder
solid sliding arc,
red, as sun
slowly setting.

Cantilever,
reach out and west,
and release my thoughts
from problems to rest.[3]

Perhaps the Invisible Bridge should attempt to emulate the delicate anatomy of this creature, and to disappear as it does when at rest upon a grass stem. It would exist as a paused, silent artwork, nestled adjacent to an existing flint and brick wall, becoming 'invisible' within the tranquil surrounding landscape until slowly projected out by turning a large-diameter handwheel connected to a rack-and-pinion drive, to finally cantilever 22 metres (72 feet) to its rock landing-pad.

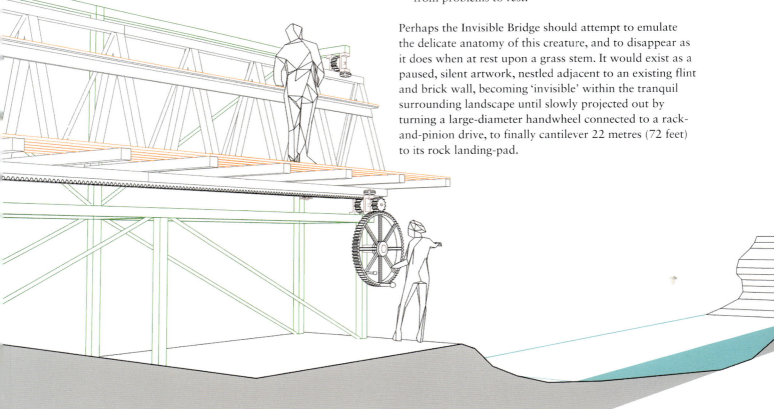

An imaginary, insubstantial folly without any evident structure apart from accumulated, unknappe

Translating Memories
This idea evoked the client's memories of gangplanks and rare escapes from the prison a boat can become. Recalling these memories in conversation segued into notions of a ghostly, sculptural third barn to complete the fourth side of a now-grassed courtyard, formed by the house and the two extant 18th-century timber barns, which was a farmyard in earlier times. Historic maps up to 1931 indicate the existence of a third barn here from the mid-1800s onwards.

What did we know about this missing barn? When was it built? What did the barn contain? What did it smell of, and what daylit atmosphere did it create?

The 1922 sale particulars included:

Large enclosed yard
Timber and thatched barn part of which contains stalls for eleven cows, also two bull pens. Brick, timber and slated barn. Range of brick and tiled cow pens for twenty nine cows and two calf pens. Dairy adjoining with brick floor.[4]

The property was sold again in 1931 and maps differ. In one the third barn is shown; in the other, the land registry map, it has vanished. It would appear that the lost barn was the *'Range of brick and tiled cow pens'*. Was it physically at the scale of the two that still exist? Unlikely. Did it go up in flames accidently or on purpose? Or did it simply become useless, and a liability to the owners? There is a trace of it revealed as a depression, slightly lower than the extant grassed courtyard.

The client agreed to the idea of a physical 'lost barn' as a way of completing the courtyard, but without losing entirely the relationship of the extant barn and grassed landscape to the River Itchen.

To reinstate a lost building in a manner that is not a replica suggests a known form, but one without a tangible structure or skeleton. A recognisable form that is structureless, and suitable for unknown activities, or imaginary uses. Time will enable these to happen, and when new people arrive they may find different ways to inhabit it. And, of course, nature will adopt it whether encouraged to do so or not.

Designing from historical notions of building typologies, while not having a programme to fulfil, releases the mind to envisage other spaces. Is it a building or a construct of the imagination?

Considering this barn is not strictly enclosing space, it is difficult to imagine privacy within it; yet neither is it a public space. It does not divide indoors from outdoors, and the walls are no barrier to the environment. It has an enigmatic appearance and questions of purpose are incidental to its scale of intention, yet through its concinnity will achieve an architectural presence. It suggests an embrace with nature, appearing to allow the landscape to flow uninterrupted through it, like the movement of air, sunlight and rain.

The Ghost Barn has openings, suggesting where doors might be, but there are none. It removes the certainty of the inside/outside duality and demands another way of looking and experiencing space. An imaginary, insubstantial folly without any evident structure apart from accumulated, unknapped pre-Neolithic field flint, shaped like bones or miniature animals, caged along its two long bases. Any one of the flints – ghost-casts of ancient, soft-bodied sea creatures' burrows – capable of becoming alive again when held or removed, especially when knapped into a sharp tool. Holding a sun-warmed or rain-wet stone surface and feeling its mass, tracing its contours with finger or palm, looking at its colours, and in the touching, holding and caressing, this tangible matter can silence memories for a moment.

Ian Ritchie,
Photograph of flint nodules, Hampshire,
England,
27 October 2023
opposite: The formation of flint is a complex process which began in the chalk seas millions of years ago. Long after knapped (split) flints were first used as tools by pre-Neolithic peoples, unknapped flint was used as a building material for its durability and aesthetic qualities. Flint walls became commonplace in southern England, and the Romans exploited its hardness and durability for roads and buildings. It is still used in walls today, and the organic shapes of flint nodules have inspired artists such as Henry Moore and Bryan Kneale.

A spherical radiolarian shell and a
Podocyrtis Ampla radiolarian
below: Flints formed within the sediment that later became chalk, formed from sea sponges and the remains of trillions of microscopic calcareous and siliceous planktonic micro-organisms (diatoms, radiolarians) during the late Cretaceous period (60 to 95 million years ago). The elaborate, airy, exquisite architecture of their globular shells has been a source of fascination for artists, architects and scientists since microscopy revealed their existence. These photographs of radiolarians show the intricate mineral skeletons of these unicellular protists of 0.1 to 0.2 millimetres.

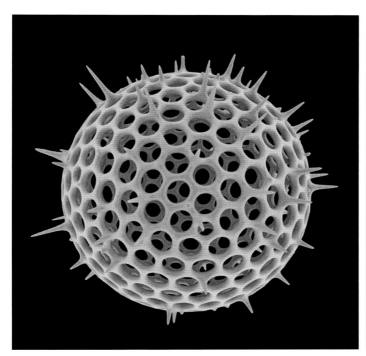

The Ghost Barn is the opposite of home, for it holds no memories

This state of the unknapped flint invokes the Japanese concept of Ma. Its kanji symbol 間 combines door 門 and sun 日: fundamental elements of architecture. Ma is the time and space life needs to breath, to feel and connect. We need time to reflect, and space to do so or we cannot grow. This was a major challenge that the client experienced in her youth while being at sea for ten years with her parents and younger brother. Experiencing all the space offered by the ocean and cosmos from the deck was her outdoor space. But it was also the cabin inside. Being trapped on a small floating prison both inside and outside makes imagination the only freedom available. This is the conceptual idea behind the Ghost Barn – to give time and space to whoever needs it, and to allow imagination to visualise the invisible.

Experiencing Ma in the West is difficult. One clue to its meaning is in theatre – a pregnant pause – when silence invades space, when there is no movement and we imagine possibilities. The same applies to music and rhetoric. Mark Twain, the famous American writer and orator, said 'No word was ever as effective as a rightly timed pause. [It] often achieves a desired effect where no combination of words howsoever felicitous could accomplish it.'[5] The Ghost Barn anticipates the beauty of silence, the cage casts shadows on itself from the sun's rays, and with luck will allow us to imagine being where we are not, in a space that gains substance from its emptiness. The seasons will change perception of the space, as it embraces nature's essential quality – change. It will no doubt create other extraordinary natural effects such as miniature snow landscapes on the ground within.

Sound represents what English musician and author David Toop has described as the presence of an absence – something that is and is not, something more than a spirit, but without a body – a ghost: 'John Cage's writings implanted (at least) two important ideas: music grows out of silence and paradoxically, there is no silence, since the sounds of the world are invasive.'[6] Silence is recognised but lies somewhere between perception and imagination and impossible to fully experience. It offers an open door into our imaginary worlds that can be both enchanting and chilling.

The Ghost Barn is the opposite of home, for it holds no memories. It cannot contain anything except the next generations' future memories of events that take place there, but only if it remains this essential space for life's other breaths.

Making Memories Tangible
A double-layer of Corten-A rods will form a bespoke 3D mesh to create imaginary walls and a roof, and is chromatically complementary to the red-brick house. The layers are tied together to create a self-supporting structure, with their bases anchored by the mass of the unknapped flint.

The mesh walls fold inwards at their base and extend to form a regular, rust-coloured grid infilled with earth and red bricks flush to the rods to create the floor. The earth, compacted as if it were from the vanished barn, loosens towards the perimeter to accept areas for planting, while the grid oversails areas of water within and without the barn, reflecting patterns of itself against the sky.

The red-brick floor infills mimic the main terrace surrounding the house, and by extending the Corten-mesh floor grid north–south towards the terrace beyond the gable-end openings, it weaves a trace of the Ghost Barn into the landscape. The pattern of brick, planting or water infilling the mesh openings will create a pathway into and through the barn.

One day the Ghost Barn may be dripping with white and/or blue wisteria, with swallows returning every year to its safety and silence. Meanwhile, it possesses a sculptural, ethereal quality of emptiness where negative spaces outweigh opaque material. That quality, combined with nature's takeover, will give it a natural beauty. ᗄ

Notes
1. Andrea Raimondi, *The Invisible Bridge Between the United Kingdom and Piedmont*, Cambridge Scholars Publishing (Newcastle upon Tyne), 2019, pp 1–2.
2. Philip Larkin, *The Complete Poems of Philip Larkin, Bridge for the Living*, ed Archie Burnett, Faber & Faber (London), 2012, p 253.
3. Poem by Ian Ritchie, 26 August 2021.
4. Savage and Weller Auctioneers and Estate Agents, *1922 Sale Particulars*, from the Hampshire County Council's Archives.
5. Mark Twain, 'Autobiographical dictation, 11 October 1907', *Autobiography of Mark Twain, Volume 3*, eds Harriet E Smith et al, University of California Press (Oakland, CA), October 2015.
6. David Toop, 'Humans, Are They Really Necessary?', in Rob Young (ed), *Undercurrents: The Hidden Wiring of Modern Music*, The Wire / Continuum International Publishing Group (London), 2002, p 125.

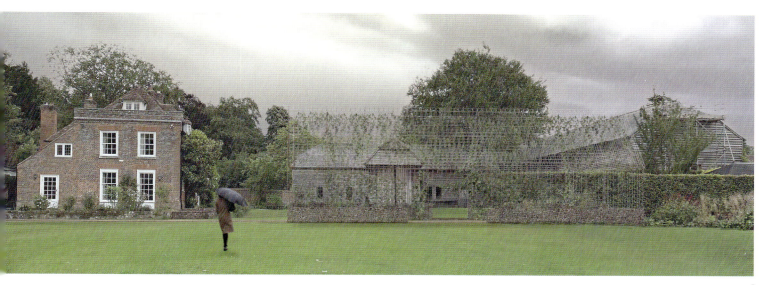

ritchie*studio,
Ghost Barn,
South Downs National Park, Twyford,
Hampshire, England,
2023

above: Architectural render of the Ghost Barn on a rainy day, viewed from the west and fabricated from Corten rod and stabilised by a flint base-fill. There are no foundations, no columns, no posts and no roof trusses, but nature can be seen through a few thousand gridded 'windows', of which each single frame is 25 x 25 centimetres (9.8 x 9.8 inches), that span the entire walls.

right: Exploded axonometric of one modular bay. The prefabrication of the barn is based on wall, roof and floor modular elements connected by Corten ties during installation. A finer-grain inner layer of Corten mesh retains the flint base-fill.

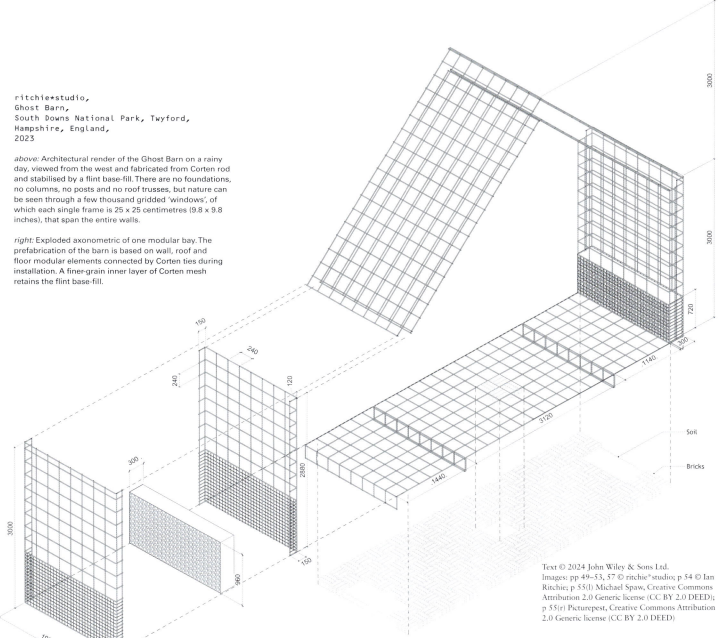

Text © 2024 John Wiley & Sons Ltd.
Images: pp 49–53, 57 © ritchie*studio; p 54 © Ian Ritchie; p 55(l) Michael Spaw, Creative Commons Attribution 2.0 Generic license (CC BY 2.0 DEED); p 55(r) Picturepest, Creative Commons Attribution 2.0 Generic license (CC BY 2.0 DEED)

Peter J Baldwin

Solid Shadows

Presencing Memory, Manifesting Memorial

Michael Sandle,
Catafalque for Anton Bruckner,
1981
Sandle's sculpture depicts a catafalque
– a raised structure used to support and
elevate a coffin during a lying in state,
funeral or memorial service – for the
19th-century Austrian composer and
organist Anton Bruckner.

Memorials operate on many semiotic and mnemonic levels, and are often created at an architectural scale constituted as clusters of artistically choreographed and architectonically situated signs and symbols. Guest-Editor of this △D **Peter J Baldwin** explores the sculptural and drawn work of Royal Academician Michael Sandle and discusses the artist's multilayered and multiscaled oeuvre that bristles with haunted, painful pasts – lest we forget!

Michael Sandle,
The Pornography of War,
2020
opposite left: One of Sandle's many portrayals of the machines of war, this drawing, a proposal for a sculpture, frames a diving fighter jet between four torches. Sandle's work often explores the disconnections and indiscriminate consequences of aerial combat, something he witnessed first-hand in the bombing of both Weymouth and Plymouth during the Blitz.

Michael Sandle,
As Ye Sow So Shall Ye Reap: An Allegory (Acknowledgements to Holman Hunt),
2015
opposite right: Inspired by English painter William Holman Hunt's allegorical painting *The Light of the World* (1853), which depicts a figure of Jesus preparing to knock at a long-disused door, this sculpture references the plight of Anwar Balousha, a Palestinian man, who had lost five of his daughters to an Israeli air strike on Gaza in 2008.

To understand our fate and theirs, we must do more than tell ghost stories. We must also tell the war stories that made ghosts and made us ghosts, the war stories that brought us here.
— Viet Thanh Nguyen, *Nothing Ever Dies: Vietnam and the Memory of War*, 2016[1]

Society, it is often claimed, is haunted. Our pasts always ever-present, projected into contemporary consciousness[2] through the milieu of the mediascape and the collective conglomeration of cultural production. From art to architecture, and from music to fiction, our sociocultural metanarratives pervasively permeate society, influencing our worldview(s) and shaping our (built) environments.

If we consider architecture to be a product of the society that constructs it, then it is almost inevitable that it will become, on some metaphysical level at least, a manifestation of these hauntological orders. Yet rarely, if ever, are such links between art and architecture, myth, media and memory made more explicit than they are in the design of a monument or a memorial. Blurring the boundaries of structure and sculpture, these complex conjunctions of signs and signifiers are shaped by our collective understanding of history and event, and mediated by our individual imaginations.

Not unlike noted French anthropologist Claude Lévi-Strauss's model of myth,[3] the creation of a memorial, and the attendant act of mourning that accompanies it, narratively reconstructs the impossible paradox of simultaneously present imagined and symbolic orders, not with the intention of resolving it but rendering it intelligible and knowable. Through this enaction we are afforded experience and understanding, not as the imparting of cold knowledge, but 'as transformative recognition'.[4]

These musings on the manifestation of memory and commemorative act of constructing a memorial are explored through the hauntings that saturate the work and workings of noted sculptor and artist Michael Sandle RA.

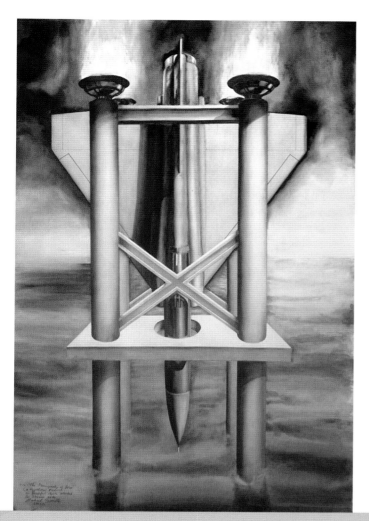

Against Heroic Decadence

Best known for his figurative sculptures, Sandle is perhaps one of the few contemporary artists with sufficient reserves of wit and courage, and the monumental rage necessary, to tackle that most emotive and complex of 21st-century subjects – the radical technologification of warfare and the inevitable and paradoxical disconnection from conflict this new machinic proliferation brings. Viewing this disconnection is an almost inevitable consequence of the perpetuation of the media, and in particular visual media's metastatic saturation with images of conflict. Sandle's work continually mediates themes of combat, inhumanity and media manipulation as he explores the heroic decadence of capitalism and its involvement in conflict at a global scale.

Yet this preoccupation with the obscenity of conflict, and the literal and metaphorical distance between combatant and victim, is not some ghoulish or perverse fetishism nor a monstrous warmongering. Educated and erudite, Sandle's work is far from an attempt to glorify war; it is instead an emotive critique and an impassioned plea against the obscene glamour that pervades our modern view and understanding of warfare.

A Culture of Fragments

To spend time with Sandle is to bear witness to the preoccupations that quite clearly haunt him. From his formative years as a boy in the port city of Plymouth on the south coast of England during the Blitz, the events of which he recounts with an almost preternatural detail, to the more recent global events that clearly provoke sadness and anger in equal measures, the germination and manifestation of his work is governed by long cycles and deep rhythms, permitting a fecund gathering of cultural fragments. From Micky Mouse to machine guns, to dive-bombing fighter jets and the bloodied figures of premiers and their slot-mouthed first ladies, Sandle's work walks a fine line between figurative and abstract representation that subverts both conventions of subject and known typologies, often resulting in uncanny and often uncomfortable juxtapositions that viscerally connect us with the subject at hand.

Michael Sandle,
Tympanum maquette,
2022
below: A small-scale maquette for the Tympanum, one of the three sculptures proposed for All Souls Masonic Lodge in Weymouth, Dorset. The figures depict a complex mixture of symbolism drawn from Weymouth's wartime and naval history; from the masonic skeleton, to GIs, to wounded soldiers and nurses to forget-me-nots and shot-down spitfires, the scene is redolent with cultural ephemera.

Michael Sandle,
Mould for *Mickey Mouse with Spikes*
(1980), photographed 2023
opposite left: The Jesmonite mould for one of Sandle's more infamous works – an interpretation of the famous Disney character adorned with BDSM (bondage and discipline, domination and submission, sadism and masochism) straps and spikes coated in a thin layer of plaster dust (itself a form of ghost of the process of mould-making and casting) – sits innocuously on a shelf in Sandle's studio.

Michael Sandle,
A New Study for the Allegory of Hope – Revised,
2023
opposite right: In more recent charcoal sketches, Sandle's original design for the statue of *Hope* (one of two statues and the Tympanum that constitute the triptych intended for the Masonic Lodge), traditionally depicted as a young maiden carrying an anchor, has become haunted by the bare-breasted aspect of Charity, this super-positioning of signifiers permitting a dual reading of the figure.

Act(ion)s *in Potentia*

From the crafting of words on the page to the smelting of the luscious bronze that so often renders Sandle's intent tangible, in the action of making, in the coming together of hand and mind there is an act of manifestation, the disclosure of a hidden truth, revealed unto the world through the generative mechanisms of poiesis (the classically understood notion of bringing into being), the interplay of imagination and the act(ion)s of artifice.

Spaces of making – sketchbooks, studios, offices, work rooms, foundries and forges – are often haunted collections of hauntological fragments, of half-formed, half-finished, half-finishable mediations of creative intent. These residues and traces sit alongside the apparatus of making, offering suggestions and hints, the ghostly traces of projects completed and forgotten, or perhaps yet unfulfilled.

Among the more recent creations and remnants that haunt Sandle's working spaces are a series of sketches, maquettes and models for a triptych of sculptural installations intended for the All Souls Masonic Lodge in Weymouth. Of significant military importance, Weymouth was one of the ports from which the D-Day landing party was launched, and was heavily bombed during the Second World War. Comprising a pair of statues and a tympanum, the set of sculptures interprets the three theological virtues: Faith, Hope and Charity. Whilst the statues of *Faith* and *Hope* follow a more traditional convention of figurative representation, in the tympanum Sandle forgoes the bare-breasted maiden that typically signifies Charity in favour of an allegorical representation reconciling charitable events from Weymouth's past; the town took in an estimated 120,000 wounded Anzacs from the Gallipoli Campaign during the First World War, and US troops who were sent to help defeat the Nazis during the Second World War. Many Americans set off from Weymouth to their certain deaths.

Hauntings and Obsessions

To view any creative work is to commune with these ghosts and spectres of the creative's act(ion)s and the hauntology of inspirations and cultural references that birthed it. Sandle's work exploits this paradoxical dualism simultaneously, parsing a projective presencing of memory as personal understanding and as a construct of public perception, and framing the hauntings of personal experience, memory, perhaps even trauma, in a gesture of disclosure, a raising of awareness with the intention of warding and warning. In visiting Sandle and his studio, we have communed with the ghosts of 65 years of creative production, and the hauntings of an obsession that began with events some eight decades hence. ◬

Notes
1. Viet Thanh Nguyen, *Nothing Ever Dies: Vietnam and the Memory of War*, Harvard University Press (Cambridge, MA), 2016, p 243.
2. Avery Gordon, *Ghostly Matters: Haunting and the Social Imagination*, University of Minnesota Press (Minneapolis, MN), 1997, p 8.
3. Claude Lévi-Strauss, *Structural Anthropology*, tr Claire Jacobson, Basic Books (New York), 1963, p 210.
4. Gordon, *op cit*, p 8.

Text © 2024 John Wiley & Sons Ltd. Images: pp 59, 61(l), 62–3(b), 63(tr) © Michael Sandle; p 61(r) Photo © Simon Stringer; p 63(tl) Photo Peter J Baldwin

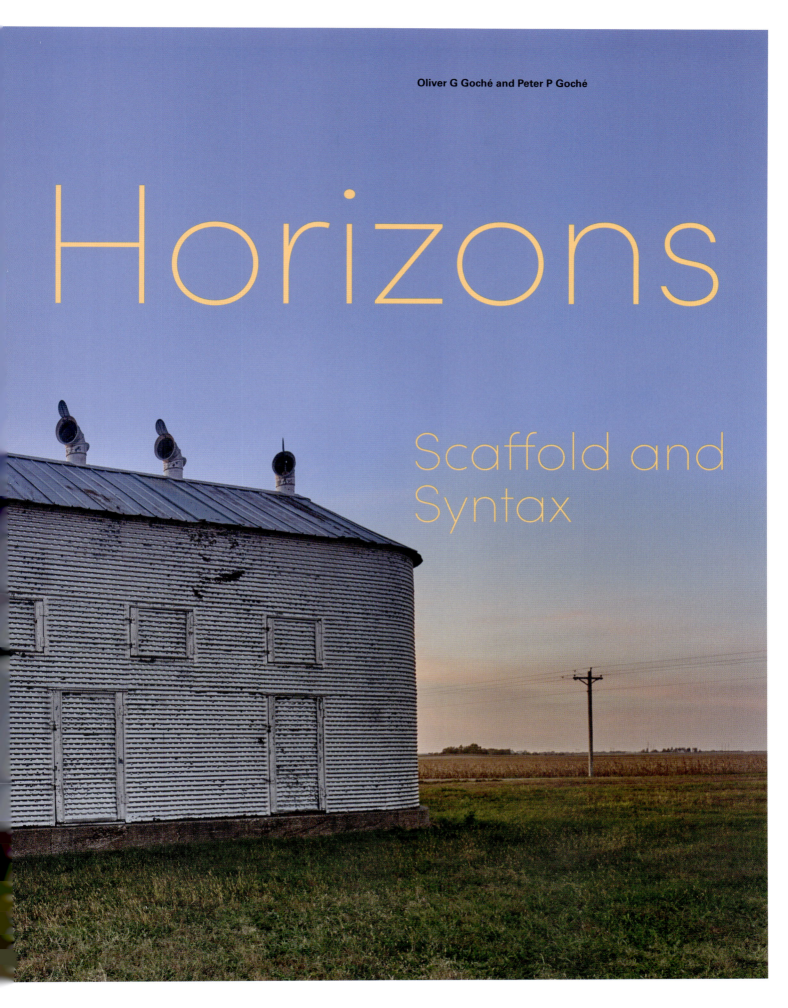

Oliver G Goché and Peter P Goché

Horizons

Scaffold and Syntax

An empty granary in Iowa proves to be an experimental laboratory for immersive performative experiences and the manifestation of ghostly apparitions and ideas. The derelict building is porous and permeable, exhibiting a certain uncanniness through the shifting register of haunting vicissitudes which can be projected on, cross-pollinated with, visually explored, touched, heard and marvelled at. Artist and designer **Oliver G Goché** and architect **Peter P Goché** take us through some of these ethereal vistas and environments.

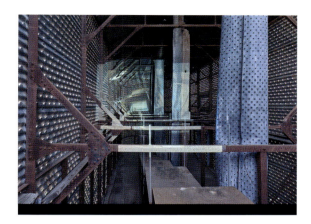

Peter P Goché,
Granary,
Napier, Iowa,
2023

previous spread: Exterior of the autonomous granary against the horizon at twilight. The soft glow of the horizon, caused by the refraction and scattering of the sun's rays from the atmosphere, tinkers with the metallic coating of this ghost vessel.

opposite left: Interior of the metal granary looking up the drawing scaffold. Installed in 2018 as part of another creative endeavour, this ascent provides multiple levels from which to attain a fragmented view of the unfolding world beyond the perforated skin of the granary. The scaffold now serves as a platform for ongoing experiments with video projection.

opposite right: The upper landing and projection platform of the drawing scaffold. The optimal elevation for viewing the distant line between earth and sky through the perforated envelope of the granary.

left: Oscillated video projection with the horizon beyond. Axial view of ghost imagery amidst the tectonic construct of the host facility animated by airborne dust particles.

Built in 1929, the metal granary manufactured by the Martin Steel Products Company in Mansfield, Ohio, is located just outside of Napier, Iowa, on a quarter section (the traditional US homestead size equating to one-fourth of a square mile) of agricultural production ground. Given the delicate structural order and array of apertures, the interior volume is unpredictable in its sensorial effects. The climatic conditions of this defunct facility offered a potent site for the creation of new atmospheric effects. It is a volumetric enclosure – a type of agricultural condenser within which we constructed a suspended drawing scaffold from which to project videos of alternative landscapes. Working in collaboration with the extant structure's past and material presence, we developed a drawing practice that would intensify the building's atmospheric complexity.

The project is an extension of an experimental drawing expedition in 2015 and subsequent collaboration with Samantha Krukowski in 2018. It builds on our ongoing investigations into the potential of the post-industrial condition as a means of internalising our intellectual comprehension of the relationships between an autonomous granary and the world at large. This projective drawing methodology has yielded a material and immaterial phenomenon that deepens our understanding of the ghost cultures that manifest themselves within the abandoned structure.

Site and Source

The granary was the primary site of investigation for three lines of enquiry. The first used projected video of oscillating light recorded at another agricultural site nearby; the second used a video recording of the Adriatic Sea with its corresponding tide and horizon; and the third documented the passage of the sun through the many perforations of the building envelope. The aim was to comprehend our inherited post-industrial landscape and the various ghost cultures that previously occupied this oblong granary. The installation of a suspended drawing scaffold from which to project videos and ascertain a view of the horizon through the perforated building envelope was critical to the project.

By grafting the past onto the present, it becomes possible to speculate on the future of the Midwestern agricultural scene. The installation of the drawing scaffold and various projections incite a dialogue about future uses and occupancies specific to drawing out the worlds *of* and *between* here and there. It makes and remakes evident its origin as it produces a trajectory towards time to come. It merges fragmented pasts and territories and consequently produces the appearance of multiple worlds in the same space.

It was within this context that episodes of experimental drawing and ghost syntax were developed. The ghost syntax are descriptors of the intangible qualities present within the granary. The qualities become heightened with the spatial assemblage and begin to relate to the stories and unseen characters of the Iowa landscape referenced in the ghost syntax. These characters, histories and narratives are cloaked in an atmosphere of sensorial conditions engendered by a series of projections and reflections.

Oscillation Chamber

Light, emanating from a video projection, strikes the varied deformation of the granary's interior surface. The video contains a recorded spatial phenomenon – daylight oscillated by a free-spinning fan into a machine shed that first served as a sorting facility for an agricultural seed-drying operation. Cast into the granary, the projection animates the oblong volume. Occupants are left to reckon the apparent mirage of the horizon as an optical illusion caused by atmospheric conditions set in motion by the video. Harvested from one post-industrial site and then inserted into this neighbouring post-industrial site, this illusion is fuelled by nearly a century's worth of dust particles captured in the rays of projected light. Shadows are eliminated and the even distribution of the flickering light softens the matrix of the host facilities' tectonic attributes. The following ghost syntax is a literary record and spatial recall:

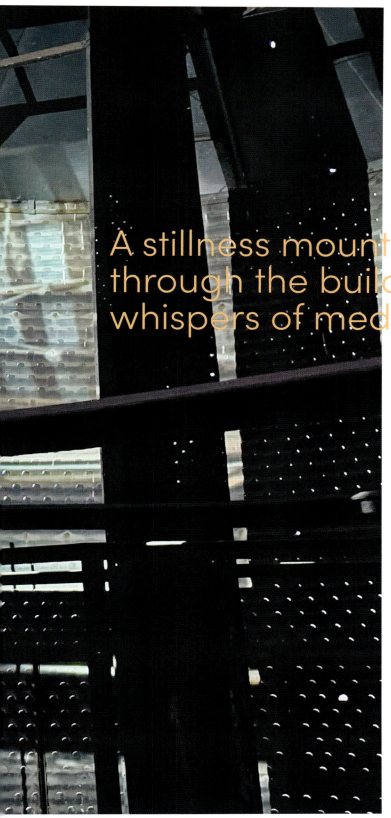

Peter P Goché,
Granary,
Napier, Iowa,
2023
Broken volumetrics with oscillated video projection. Off-axis image of the complexity of building elements and projection at twilight. A new ghost complexity emerges because of the host granary tectonics and the video subject tectonics.

A stillness mounts as the wind sifts through the building's skin offering whispers of meditation and meander

It is here that the body is enveloped by space – amid the incessant visual rotation and almost inaudible silence. Our conscious is distorted by the wafting cycles of source and host. A stillness mounts as the wind sifts through the building's skin offering whispers of meditation and meander. With a conceited grin we are both reminded of Juhani Pallasmaa's eyes of the skin.[1] It's an amusing thing – this newfound draughtsmanship provides a profound chuckle as we trace the spatial configuration with bare foot and pause intermittently to press our ear to the perforated skin in effort to sense that which lies beyond. The roof diaphragm clatters as the environment beyond is strained and now occupies the pulp of our minds. And now, we are caught inside the metaphysical constraints of this pendulum timepiece as two angels descend upon a body lying in the trench. The corpse is wrapped in layers of linen bandages covered with a resinous coating and entombed in an aura of time as we bear witness to the distinctive atmosphere that surrounds and is seemingly generated by the mummified body. Sealed with a whisper of the breeze sifting through the building, the angels ascend while we sit knees in arms at the top of the scaffold and watch on. We sit motionless as the building envelope begins to weep. Our bodies are now in sync with mother nature's slow, rhythmic secretions.

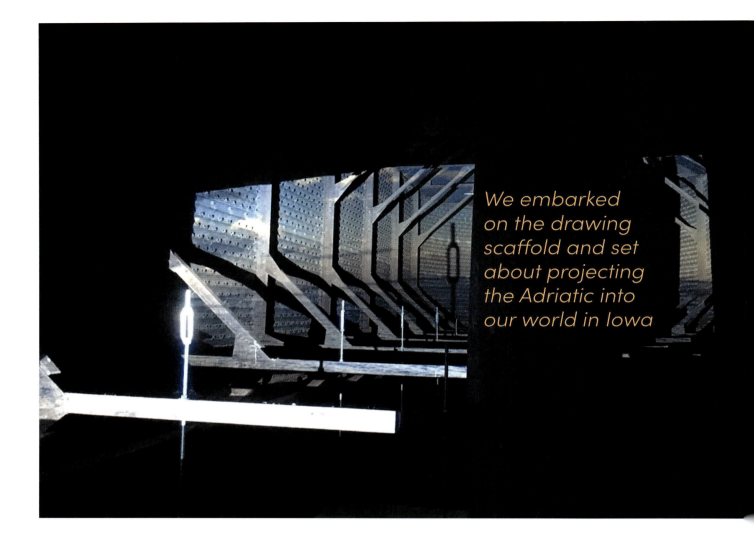

We embarked on the drawing scaffold and set about projecting the Adriatic into our world in Iowa

Adriatic Sea
The Adriatic Sea, noted for its stunning blue and green hues, is the northernmost arm of the Mediterranean Sea and has been a cultural crossroads for centuries. For a similar timeframe, it has served as the primary shipping port for the Italian and Balkan peninsulas. Videographic possibilities were sought on our trip to Venice in 2018. Sitting on Venice's Lido, we were overwhelmed with the incessant repetition of the rising and falling of the sea due to the attraction of the moon and sun – it consumed our consciousness. The following hours were spent capturing these phenomena on video. Recalling this footage a few years later, we sourced a 22-second clip, an at-grade video, that illustrated our memory of the specific sensory engagement with the Adriatic. We embarked on the drawing scaffold and set about projecting the Adriatic into our world in Iowa. By aligning the horizon line of the Adriatic with that of Iowa as well as the tectonic components of the granary, we constructed a new world and auric index. This assembly drew on and conflated two disparate spaces and cultures separated by 5,000 miles. The interior of the metal vessel became the canvas onto which a place halfway around the world was redrawn.

Belief and disbelief at sea, we stumble and stammer in shallow waters as the lunar pull swells and contracts along the horizon. The line at which the sea and sky appear to meet shines with a soft tremulous light. Alternating rise and fall of the sea waters against contracted grounds arrest our gaze as we lay inebriated along its edge. Lulled by the tide, we drift off into daydreams and fleeting memories of the old country as a cloud of atmosphere forms overhead. Ingested by our subconscious, we shift to the foetal position in the absence of our shadow as the low frequency of the

water slowly rises over the shore and then slowly falls back again. With the arrival of a Great Horned Owl our return to conscious is announced by the 'hooo, hoo, hoo' vocalisations we studied with our mother in the middle of the night. Consumed by darkness and washed up in the gentle caress of the Midwestern starry night we slouch on all fours and lower our heads to the trench and inhale the fog beneath our arrival. The vanishing of the sea happens as we bear witness to the technological marvel of the uncountable obscura. This vanishing is as unsolved as it is fabulous. And is as unheard of as it is lovely. It is something dreamt about and talked about in whispers and then promptly forgotten. It, by no means, is consequential to the lifecycle of the horizon, merely a blink, on its unceasing march.

Peter P Goché,
Granary,
Napier, Iowa,
2023

opposite: The horizon of the Adriatic Sea contained within the granary. Axial perspective of video projection as the advancing seawater strikes the regularly spaced collar ties of the host facility. The ghost horizon of the Adriatic is aligned with Iowa's horizon seen through the host faculties' perforated skin.

above: Off-axis perspective of video projection at nightfall. The ghostly tide of the Adriatic Sea seemingly floats amidst an apparition of emptiness as the scene of the video strikes the granary's structural skeleton.

Through focused observation, we experienced a heightened awareness of the passing of time as the cosmic pattern of sunlight crept along its daily course

Camera Obscura

In the transitional months of spring and autumn we could enter the granary and witness a phenomenological event whereby the many perforations in the building's skin act as a series of pinhole cameras through which an image of the sun appears in the space. The consequent apparition of multiple suns radiates throughout the space, illuminating the concrete trench and floor, the disfigured vent shafts, folded scaffold, corrugated skin and oxidised building frame. Through focused observation, we experienced a heightened awareness of the passing of time as the cosmic pattern of sunlight crept along its daily course.

In a luxurious hunger, we orbit with bloated bellies about ten thousand suns. We sit single file along the drawing scaffold as the school of solar projections bathe our skin and bone. Beyond, we hear the rustle of the 120-acre expanse of cornfield. Further beyond, we catch murmurs from *Techniques of the Observer*[2] and broken notes on the camera obscura by Jonathan Crary. Inside this pinhole camera we are arrested by the projection of the many worlds beyond. The blur of the illuminated creep absolves us of our ecology. Meanwhile, our bodies resonate from a more localised percussion just outside the granary's perforated metal jacket as the Great Plains Action Society chant 'no CAFOs, no BIG-AG, no GMOS – Decolonise farming'. With a solemn silence, the chains of the weary clang. They bear the colours of the forgotten and meander a dusty route. They scream out towards the heavens in search of something not quite certain as they approach the 1,000 apertures. A different being beckons in towards the perforated expanse and sounds the sounds of the earth. The weary begins to climb towards the heavens, toward where it screams. They are still uncertain. Their uncertainty drives them higher and higher still as they recite the prose of their memory until finally, they reach the top. They look out amongst the onlookers, acknowledging, but also not, their presence, and take one last long look at them before turning towards the heavens, finally. They unknowingly look towards the heavens and through a singular aperture close their eyes.

This series of three ghost syntax, in addition to the drawing scaffold and consequent projections, produced a type of spatial atmosphere and historical occupation. Each experimental visit provided a new way to survey our story line. This obscured way of seeing allowed us to contemplate history and the material leftovers, a medium that does not conform to contemporary culture and the resulting atmospheric yield.

Reflection

Architecture is the archaeological measure of past civilisations. Our impression of such matter depends on the manners and techniques employed by those who excavate its context. Each drawing expedition serves as a material conflation that yielded a specific aesthetic experience that is no longer a single continuum but rather a multilayered terrain of otherness. The drawing methodology produced alternative ways to reconceptualise the nature of this post-industrial space.

As experimentalists, the process of surveying vacant constructs tends to have less to do with a specific former function and more to do with a heightened experiential occupation. Each architectural conversion is contingent on what might be referred to as depth, which is not a dimension, as such, but rather the embodiment of depth and breadth. This set of material and immaterial conditions are manifestations of discontinuity and difference that yield an atmospheric equilibrium steeped in the past and haunted by the present. In the dormancy of our cultural foundation, we are baptised in the accumulation of past occupations. We submit – laying down our perceptual being before the audible latency of world histories. Standing erect with our arms by our sides, we embody the metallic songs of the past with a relative capacity to unite and interact with the gentle sheen of the inherited landscape. A perpetual wind continues to sift and howl through the obsolete repository for grain (geographical coordinates: 41o98', 93o64'). ⌂

Notes
1. Juhani Pallasmaa, *The Eyes of the Skin*, John Wiley & Sons (Hoboken, NJ), 1996.
2. Jonathan Crary, *Techniques of the Observer*, MIT Press (Cambridge, MA), 1992.

Peter P Goché,
Granary,
Napier, Iowa,
2023

A thousand suns appear through the perforated building envelope of the granary. As the sun passes from east to west during the winter months, the solar array is accompanied by the haunting chill of the frozen landscape and distant horizon.

Text © 2024 John Wiley & Sons Ltd. Images: pp 64–5, 67, 72 © Cameron Campbell; p 66 © Assassi Productions; pp 68–71 © Peter P Goché

Nat Chard

CHASING

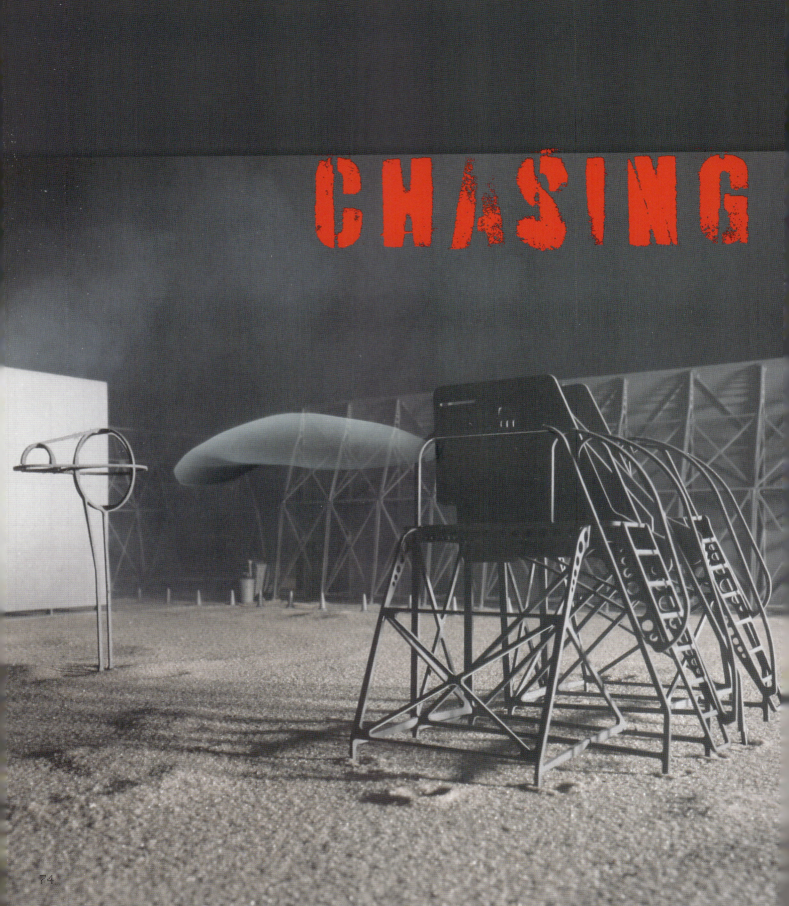

Nat Chard,
Institute of Paradoxical Shadows Research Field with mischievous floating shadows,
2023
Stereoscopic photograph/drawing with floating shadows.

PARADOXICAL SHADOWS

Shadows bring a sense of animated vitality to any building, and their representations on drawings add a sense of depth and believability to that which is being illustrated. **Nat Chard**, Professor of Experimental Architecture at University College London (UCL), has a longstanding interest in movement, optics, photography and the intangible spaces in between them. His Institute of Paradoxical Shadows cleaves the shadow from its material datum, leaving it hanging, a suspended spectral entity, encountered through a séance-like trance of cognitive confusion.

Nat Chard,
Instrument Six,
2009
Built to study the discovery of how to float shadows in mid-air, Instrument Six works both with direct viewing and in photographic mode.

The performance of light and shadow is so reliable and unerring that architects have employed shadows to animate their buildings and, in their drawings, to articulate the form of their architecture. As we are so familiar with the performance of shadows, when we see a drawing, whether an absolute projection (such as a plan or section) or a relative one (such as a perspective), faithfully drawn shadows will help the observer recognise depth in an image rendered on a flat plane. As the artist John Holmes explains in his manual *Sciagraphy* (1952), 'The elevation of any architectural form in line has the disadvantage of showing only the conventional pattern of the form as if seen with the eye opposite to each point simultaneously. Even when a plan is added it is only the practised observer who can readily conceive the solid three-dimensional form so expressed. It is by the contrast of light and shade that the eye understands solidity.'[1]

We normally experience shadows either cast onto or attached to a surface. When we see a shadow in a drawing we therefore assume not only that it lies on a surface but also that a surface exists to receive the shadow. A chance discovery of a method of floating shadows in mid-air provides the means to achieve the perversion of the shadow's normally reliable and respectable behaviour. This involves the use of polarised light to allow a separate register of the shadow for each eye to create a stereoscopic illusion of the shadow sitting in space, detached from the surface on which we would expect it to land.

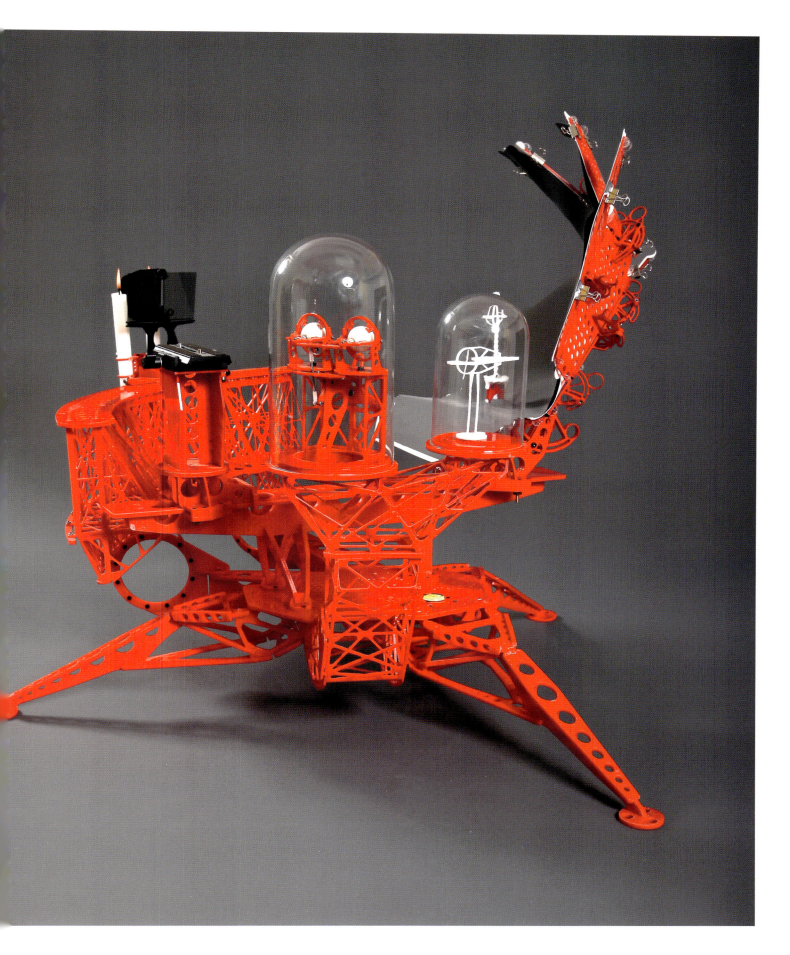

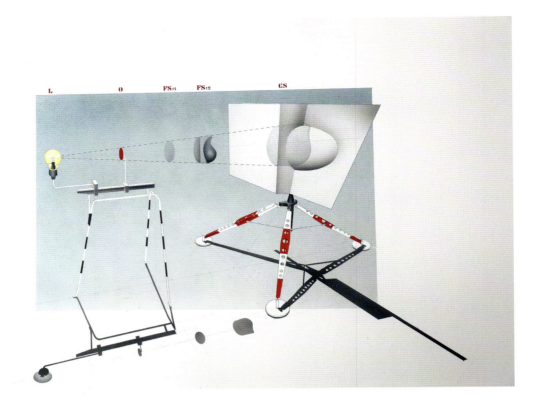

THE SHADOW IS AN AGENT OF CONVERSATION

I created Instrument Six (2009) to support the study of this discovery. To float the shadows, the light sources consist of two candles behind polarising filters. These cast the shadow of an object onto a screen that retains the polarisation of the light, so that when the observer uses glasses with polarising filters aligned with those for the corresponding candle for each eye, the object's shadow appears to float. The parallax of the two shadows seen as a single entity can position the shadow as if floating in space. The low level of illumination provided by the candlelight through the filters makes a strong enough shadow for our perception to register that it is floating in space, but weak enough so that our consciousness, which knows that shadows should land on a surface, will try to place the shadow on the surface of the screen. While observing the instrument in this configuration it is possible to choose between one's perception and consciousness to realise the position of the shadow. In conventional drawings, whether absolute or relative, we also read shadows as if they register on a surface. It is therefore only possible to recognise a floating shadow, either in person or through representation, through stereoscopic perception, and therefore much of the project is drawn stereoscopically.

Experiencing the Floating Shadow

To study the space between the perception of a floating shadow and the screen on which we would expect it to land – and to see if the pull of our consciousness is adjusting the geometric position of the shadow – Instrument Nine (2013) calibrates the position of the floating shadow. The instruments illuminate the sort of disturbance a floating shadow can cause, yet they are still captive to many of the geometric prescriptions that keep normal shadows so obedient and reliable. While it is thrilling to observe a shadow floating in front of you as if you could reach out and grasp it, the conceptual performance of the instruments is still limited by the same obstinacy of physics that makes floating shadows so disturbing in the first place. The work that forms the subject of this article is therefore developed through representation rather than demonstrations.

One of the reasons the shadow has a powerful hold on our imagination is that it articulates relationships. A cast shadow requires a light source, a subject to illuminate and an object on which its shadow is cast. In the Dutch artist Johannes Vermeer's painting *The Guitar Player* (c 1672), the shadow cast by the player's chin on her neck provides a darkness into which the same light that causes the shadow can reflect off her green dress to colour the parts in shadow. The shadow is an agent of conversation confirming how the parts are assembled. When Peter Pan's shadow becomes detached, this assembly is broken and the shadow switches from confirming his

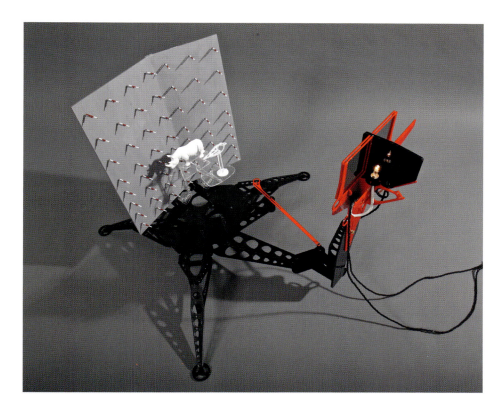

Nat Chard,
Instrument Nine,
2013
left: When viewing floating shadows from Instrument Six with candle illumination, one's perception would float the shadow in mid-air but one's consciousness would try to place it on the surface on which it would normally land. Instrument Nine was made to calibrate the position of the floating shadow to study how it was pulled by these two forces.

Nat Chard,
Atlas of Floating Shadows,
2019
opposite: Instrument Nine also examined how the form of the screen had a consequence on the form of a floating shadow. This drawing discusses the difference between a floating shadow that is independent of the screen and one whose form has been contaminated by the screen.

presence to questioning the nature of his presence. The reliability of how shadows perform and how we understand that performance makes them a suitable vehicle to discuss questions of how we construct realities, as in the Allegory of the Cave from Plato's *Republic* (*c* 375 BC).[2]

The invention of photography, a medium that initially appeared utterly truthful, encouraged proponents of phantasmagorical phenomena to employ photographs as reliable evidence of ghostly happenings. As many of the images produced in spirit photography gave away the fallibility of the medium, later exponents employed stereoscopic photography to bolster their credibility. As well as presenting a three-dimensional representation of the phenomena, the rigours of stereoscopy made it harder to fake events through post-production. In the US in 1925 there were stereoscopic photographs by RW Conant and a photographer noted simply as 'Gerke' revealing ectoplasm produced by the Boston-based medium Mina 'Margery' Crandon, and simultaneously in Canada the medical doctor Thomas Glendenning Hamilton used at least three stereoscopic cameras in his rack of photographic equipment installed to witness a range of phantasmagorical events in a room he set aside for séances. Now that we are familiar with the digital manipulation of images and with AI-generated imagery, any picture that shows a condition out of the ordinary is treated with suspicion.

The Institute of Paradoxical Shadows
The stereoscopic images of the Institute of Paradoxical Shadows that show shadows floating in space are made with the recognition that no one will imagine them to be realities. There is no attempt to pretend or to persuade that these shadows are real. There are various categories of floating shadow. Some of them can be generated in an illusory way to view directly, and these fall into two sub-categories, as illustrated in the *Atlas of Floating Shadows* (2019) – those that take the form of the shadow maker but are unsullied by the surface on which they should, by rights, land, and those that have taken the form of that surface. When viewed stereoscopically these shadows make sense, at least on their own terms. Either as flat or three-dimensional projections of the figure from which they are cast, they appear as either a shadow that has not yet reached its destination or one that has and then bounced back off that surface towards the origin. These floating shadows have an aura of logic about them and establish an introduction to the less fathomable entities that appear to be like the shadows we know yet without their logic. Instead, they are conceptual projections that do not follow our understanding of optics, like the apparitions we call ghosts.

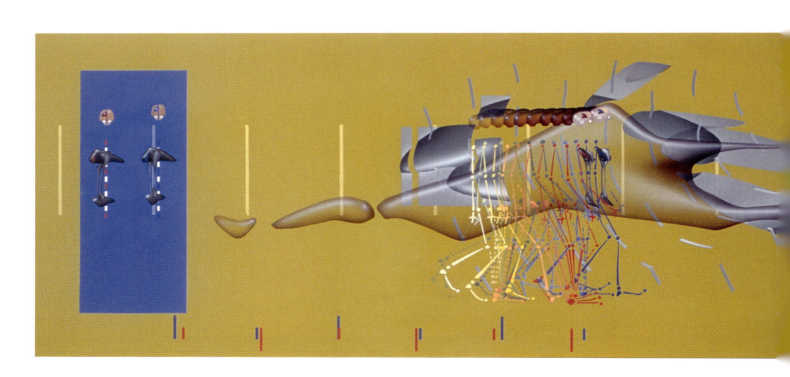

Nat Chard,
Relative projection drawing,
1993
A personal sense of how the space in
the drawing below is projected.

Such emanations appear in many of the drawings that pre-empt the work in this article – attempts to discuss an idea that often has no name and even less of an explanation, but the character of the shadow has some capacity to visually articulate a tacit idea. Two early examples are illustrated in a drawing of the imagined intimate personal space of two people walking and the associated overdrawing of a Polaroid transfer of an X-ray venturing how one of those people might imagine they are projecting such a space (both 1993). There are many other examples and they encourage confidence that such a practice can discuss ungraspable ideas. In religious paintings we see all sorts of emanations such as halos or, as in Paolo Veronese's *The Adoration of the Kings* (1573), a celestial light that is independent of our normal experience of lights that appear from the sky. More particular to the content under discussion in this article, the fluidic photography of Hippolyte Baraduc, mostly from the 1890s, purports to depict images of the human soul.[3] Baraduc was a physician at the Salpêtrière Hospital in Paris where he had studied under the neurologist and professor of anatomical pathology Jean-Martin Charcot. He specialised in nervous disorders and his fluidic photography was contemporary with the German engineer and physicist Wilhelm Conrad Röntgen's discovery of X-rays in 1895. If X-rays could see into the physical body, Baraduc's fluidic photographs venture images of the body's essential interior. The interest in this work is not the credibility of these images to depict the human soul, but their capacity to venture ideas about the presence of such an ungraspable entity.

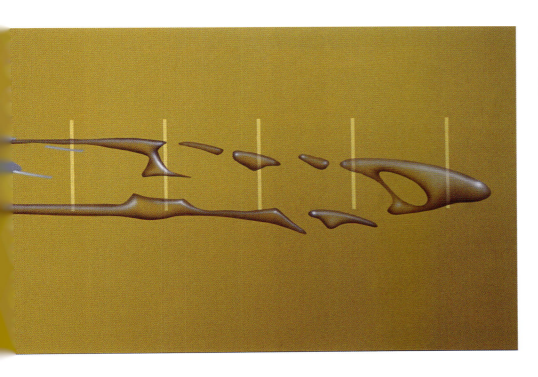

Nat Chard,
*Composite of Perceptions,
Imaginations, Memory and
Consciousness,*
1993
Composite drawing of multiple imagined sensations between two people walking.

Nat Chard,
Institute of
Paradoxical Shadows
Research Field with
floating shadows,
2023
right: Stereoscopic
photograph/drawing.

The Institute of Paradoxical Shadows is a site to play out the potential of the floating shadow as a means of discussing otherwise intangible ideas about the relational structures of architecture. The research field is made of simple elements, the arrangement partly inspired by the French physiologist Étienne-Jules Marey's architecture of shadows from his laboratories at the Collège de France in Paris, where in the 1880s he pioneered methods of chronophotography to study human and animal motion. Like film sets that are built to appear as a familiar thing yet also designed to support the needs of the film's narrative, the architectural elements in the Institute of Paradoxical Shadows research field are made to look purposeful yet to register three-dimensional information in a legible way so that the stereoscopic images make sense. In the project's earlier stereoscopic drawings that combine photographic and drawn material, 5-by-4-inch Polaroid transfers were used as the base for the work. This size can be resolved with or without lorgnettes to see the stereo images but provides a limited area on which to draw. The series is drawn and viewed with the help of mirror stereoscopes of the type used to analyse aerial photography, which allow each of the two images to be up to 250 millimetres square. As with my earlier drawing instruments, the presence of this apparently scientific apparatus not only facilitates the three-dimensional image but also might seduce the observer to take interest in the work.

The shadows in the stereoscopic images range from the normal obedient type we are used to, overlayed with logical floating

Nat Chard,
Institute of Paradoxical Shadows
Research Field, aerial view, with
orthodox floating shadow,
2023

below: Stereoscopic photograph/drawing showing projection of paradoxical shadow and latent floating shadows. To view in 3D, go cross-eyed and concentrate on the middle of the three images that appear. Try to resolve identical features from the left and right images over each other. When you resolve the image, try to hold it and wait for the depth to improve.

shadows as described earlier, to then more mischievous varieties that float out of time and out of place with their origin. The former two types of shadow are captive to the geometry of the figure from which they are cast and the light source from which they are projected, but the mischievous shadows show no respect for prescribed geometries and instead are formed by ideas (but not the form) of situation and circumstance. △

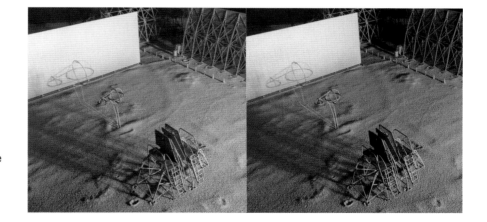

Notes
1. John M Holmes, *Sciagraphy*, Sir Isaac Pitman & Sons, London, 1952, p 1.
2. Plato, *Republic*, Oxford University Press (Oxford), 2008 edn, p 240.
3. See Hippolyte Baraduc, *The Human Soul: Its Movements, Its Lights, and the Iconography of the Fluidic Invisible*, Librairie Internationale de la Pensée Nouvelle (Paris), 1913 (first English edn) and reprinted by Andesite Press – no date given.

Text © 2024 John Wiley & Sons Ltd.
Images © Nat Chard

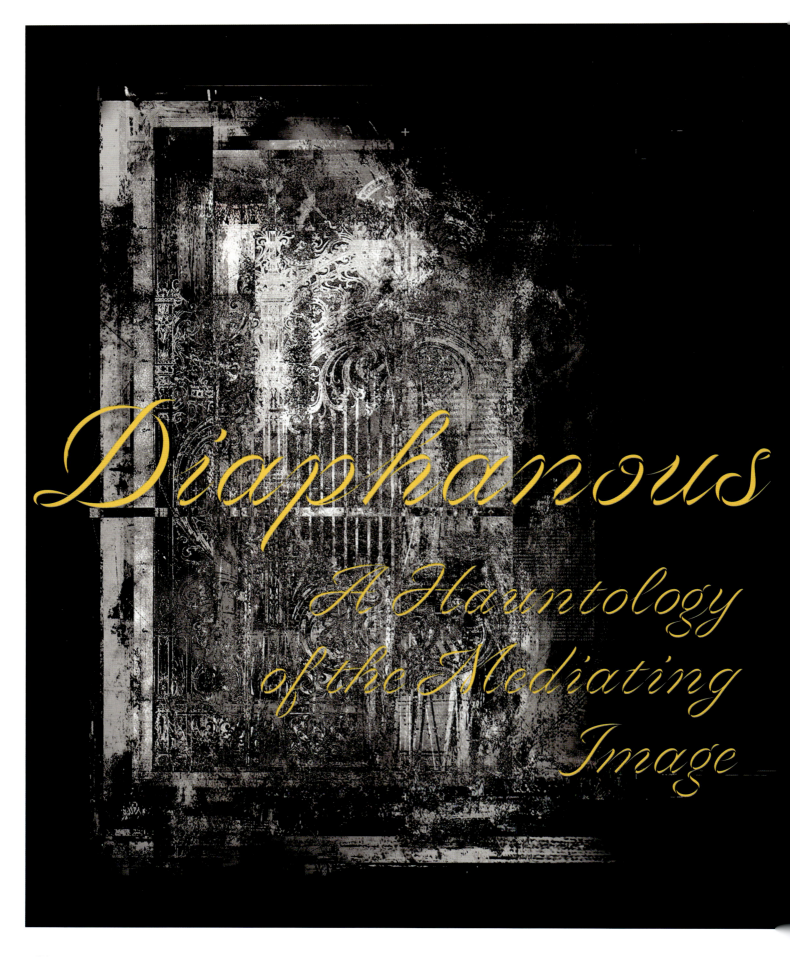

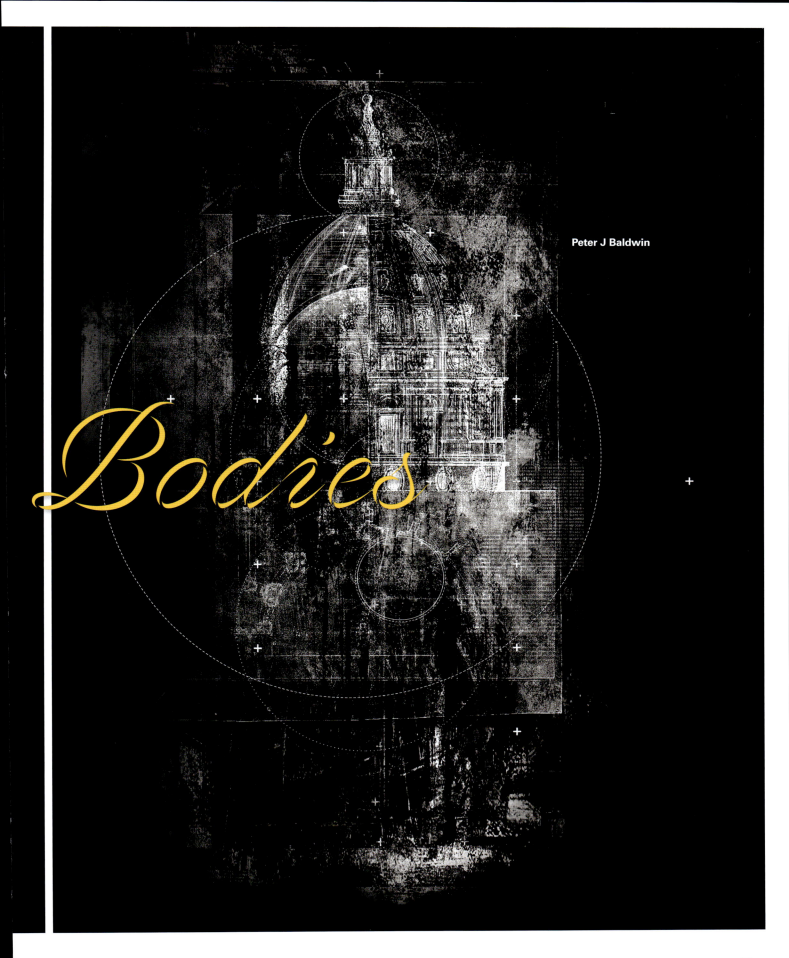

Bodies

Peter J Baldwin

The contemporary world is so dependent on the virtual, with its constantly morphing and invisibly magical potentialities, that it is somewhat paradoxical that the speculative, explorative aspect of architectural drawing is so undervalued in this context. The profession's computerised quick-fix, feed-me, satisfy-me normative mentality has limited truck with the intangible. **Peter J Baldwin** writes an ode to the phantasmagorical and the ephemeral, citing it as a useful tool to enhance and liberate the creative design mind. Allied with tactics of re-reading and post-rationalisation, he constructs a spectral 'machine' for making work.

Do you not feel that invisible presences have more reality than visible ones? They exert more influence upon us, they make us cry more easily…"
— Angela Carter, *The Infernal Desire Machines of Dr Hoffman*, 1974[1]

From the oneiric beatifications of saints to Les Grands Transparents[2] of Surrealist art and fiction, phantasmagoria have long been considered agents of disclosure, prompting, perhaps provoking creative revelation and (divine) inspiration. Poised on the cusp of sensory confusion, these spiralling sequences of hauntological ephemera, memetic fragments and poietic figments provide fertile ground for the imagination, connecting our (sub)conscious minds to a reality unbound by the limited and limiting notions of conception and perception, the confines of chronological linearity revealing deeper meaning(s) and unveiling hidden truth(s).

Aided and abetted by a web of poetic conceits, artistic provocations and philosophical prompts, my ongoing experimental design project 'Filigreed Gods – Diaphanous Bodies and Sacred Vessels' seeks, among other things, to explore the disjunctions between contemporary thinking and historical understandings of the communicative, and the mediatory functions of architectural space and representational practices. It aims to challenge our contemporary biases through the construction of a dialectic epistemology and a heuristic system of representations, tentatively referred to as the 'phantasmagorical drawings'. This emerging practice posits the reconceptualisation of the architectural drawing as heir to the long tradition of the mediating image in an effort to counter the instrumentality that has come to dominate our contemporary disciplinary discourse.

An (In)tangible Intermediary
Architecture, it might be argued, is not a physical thing, lacking fixed substance, quantifiable mass or empirical metric; its existence is contingent on the manifestation of its phenomena. Not unlike the phantom or spectre, irrespective of the media through which it manifests itself, architecture is brought into being

Peter J Baldwin,
The Great Portal of Snoutfigs, 'Filigreed Gods – Diaphanous Bodies and Sacred Vessels',
2021
previous spread, left: Inspired by French symbolist author Alfred Jarry's surreal vision of Paris described in his novel *The Exploits and Opinions of Dr Faustroll, Pataphysician* (1911), the drawing appropriates the French architect Charles Girault's design for the 'Iron door' for the Petit Palais in Paris (construction 1896–1900) as its point of departure. It constructs multiple simultaneous versions of the door predicated on an insertion into a new, narrative context to provoke considerations of the multifarious meanings and manifestations of threshold.

Peter J Baldwin,
Cogitations of the Marine Bishop Mendacious, 'Filigreed Gods – Diaphanous Bodies and Sacred Vessels',
2021
previous spread, right: Following Sir Christopher Wren's studies for the design for the Dome of St Paul's Cathedral in London (constructed 1675–1710), the drawing synthesises the architect's numerous different design proposals in an attempt to discover the original 'diagram' of architectural intent, whilst also recording the traces of its own construction.

through the conjunction of conception and perception, inherently implicating an observer in the construction of architectural experience and meaning.

Yet while other creative disciplines have embraced the ephemeral, the fluidity and phantasmagoria of contemporary (incorpo)reality, architecture, once our mediating link between the tacit and tangible, has been stripped bare, becoming increasingly fixated on matters corporeal to define its operational remit and working parameters. This is flattening architectural discourse, robbing it of its capacity to engage in a broader system of semiotics and cultural values. It denies architecture's very nature, its manifestation through the interplay of presence and absence, the mediation of tacit and tangible.

Divided Representation(s)
As with any discipline, architecture has over the course of centuries developed any number of epistemological models and representations. While some emphasise grounding, verifiability and clarity, others have sought to cultivate serendipity, objective chance and the off-kilter. Irrespective of bias, drawing has long been synonymous with architectural practice, as a critical tool and a speculative environment. Not only a means of thinking, exploring and generating new understandings and insights, it is also our primary means of communication, the projective agent of architectural intent.

Peter J Baldwin,
The Temple of Love,
'Filigreed Gods – Diaphanous Bodies and Sacred Vessels',
2023
above: The drawing is inspired by one of the many scenes from the *Hypnoerotomachia Poliphili*, written in 1499 by the mysterious Italian priest Francesco Colonna, in which the novel's protagonist Poliphilo glimpses the plan for a gnomic garden awaiting him at the end of a barren corridor whilst in pursuit of his love Polia. It begins to construct a series of key signifiers and architectural components to evoke atmosphere as much as spatial configuration.

Peter J Baldwin, *The Sealed Palace, within which the unforeseen beast Clinamen waits, whilst above the Painting Machine, suspended within a system of weightless springs, revolves in azimuth*, 'Filigreed Gods – Diaphanous Bodies and Sacred Vessels', 2022

left: The linguistic provocations and narrative prompts that saturate this work are drawn from sources many and varied and often promiscuously mixed. They frequently reference works depicting the uncanny and surreal, interpreted both literally and allegorically. Here Clinamen, the notion of unpredictability, is represented in its dual aspect as both a machinic contrivance and a gestatory environment, disrupting the classical architectural protocols into which it is inserted.

these 'diaphanous bodies', are powered by a yearning

While it is perhaps unsurprising that the 'information age' has been unkind in its treatment of the unknown, uncertain and unverified, it is not without irony that in an era characterised by digital dematerialisation, immersive media and the para-fictional hauntings of synthetic reality, phantasmagoria, those uncertain emissaries of imaginative potential, have been cast as unwelcome visitors. The new brief for architectural representation is ease of recognition and rapidity of assimilation.

Driven by the polar and polarising effects of reductive instrumentalism and aesthetic fetishisation, we have lost sight (or should that be site?) of the conditions of uncertainty that provide a home for the imaginative and imaginary devices that nourish the creative imagination, and yet this disappearance of architectural potential is often masked by the appearance of a 'sign' of architecture.[3] We assume, (in)correctly, that the representation of the exteriority of architecture (a building form) automatically implies the existence of its interiority.

This transforms our engagement with the drawing. No longer considered a critical and reflective process; something which requires time, effort and perhaps a certain degree of speculation and willingness, has been replaced by a voyeuristic desire for instant gratification.

Filigreed Gods
The cost of this pornographic instantaneity is steep, fundamentally shifting our approach to the acquisition of knowledge and the development of ideas. As we focus on recognition, we forfeit the opportunity for serendipitous insights and deeper understandings that are inherently part of the reciprocity of the drawing process.

Conceptualising the 'phantom' as a deconstructive gesture and an interstitial third state that exists between interiority and exteriority within Jacques Derrida's double system of meaning,[4] the 'Filigreed Gods – Diaphanous Bodies and Sacred Vessels' phantasmagorical drawings build on a speculative trajectory set out by noted architectural theorist and historian Dalibor Vesely, reframing the architectural drawing as a host for the intangible, the latent and the uncertain through the creation of multiplicity, simultaneity and fluidic fragmentation.[5]

The cultivation of the desired condition is not a simple task, anticipating a form of representation that actively resists a singular reading and interpretation while making visible, or at least partially visible, those things that would normally be hidden from view.

Poised on the Moment of Becoming
Existing as the conjunction of visual phenomena and abstract conceptualisation, the phantom occupies an ambiguous territory of dialectical tension, negotiating an impossible exchange through its simultaneous presence and absence.

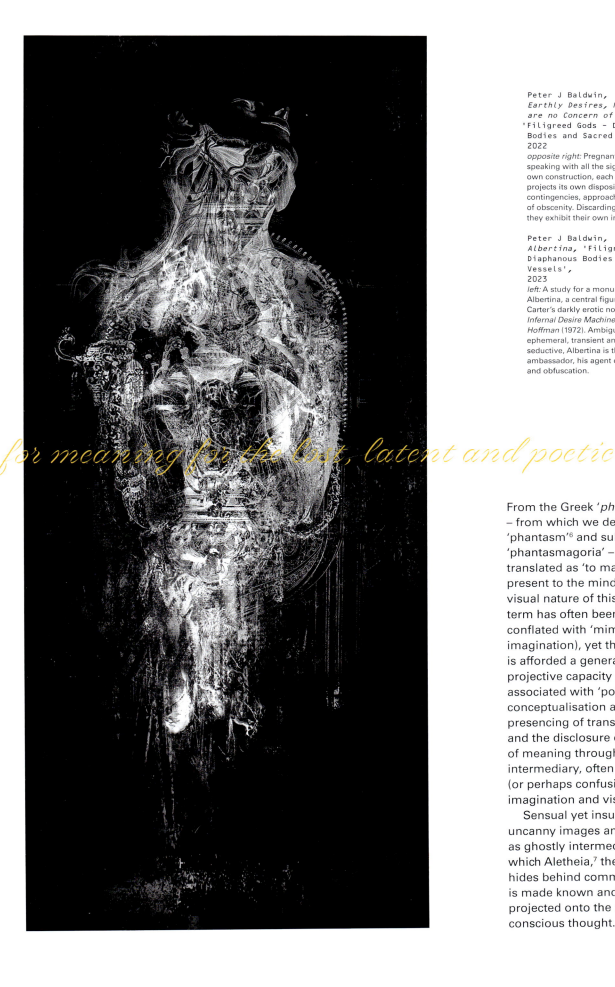

Peter J Baldwin,
Earthly Desires, Metaphysics are no Concern of Mine,
'Filigreed Gods – Diaphanous Bodies and Sacred Vessels',
2022
opposite right: Pregnant, symbolically speaking with all the signs of their own construction, each study projects its own dispositions and contingencies, approaching the point of obscenity. Discarding contention they exhibit their own inhibitions.

Peter J Baldwin,
Albertina, 'Filigreed Gods – Diaphanous Bodies and Sacred Vessels',
2023
left: A study for a monument to Albertina, a central figure in Angela Carter's darkly erotic novel *The Infernal Desire Machines of Doctor Hoffman* (1972). Ambiguous, ephemeral, transient and achingly seductive, Albertina is the Doctor's ambassador, his agent of disclosure and obfuscation.

for meaning for the lost, latent and poetic

From the Greek '*phantázō*', 'phantasia' – from which we derive 'phantom', 'phantasm'[6] and subsequently 'phantasmagoria' – might best be translated as 'to make (appear/visible) present to the mind'. Owing to the visual nature of this disclosure, the term has often been erroneously conflated with 'mimesis' (artistic imagination), yet the 'phantasm' is afforded a generative and projective capacity more commonly associated with 'poiesis' (making). Its conceptualisation alludes to a pre-presencing of transcendental signifiers and the disclosure of hidden orders of meaning through an (in)tangible intermediary, often the interplay (or perhaps confusion) of memory, imagination and vision.

Sensual yet insubstantial, these uncanny images and apparitions act as ghostly intermediaries, through which Aletheia,[7] the esoteric truth that hides behind common conception, is made known and intelligible, projected onto the medium of conscious thought. It is from this

Peter J Baldwin,
From Across Foliated Space,
'Filigreed Gods – Diaphanous
Bodies and Sacred Vessels',
2022
left: Dreams and desires, composed of fundamental signs and symbols, earthly and unearthly truths – a study for one of the 12 hairy shrines of the Universal Church of lust described in Angela Carter's *The Infernal Desire Machines of Doctor Hoffman* (1972).

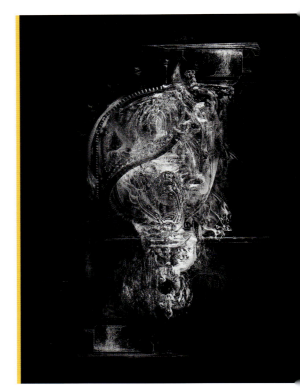

primordial fusion, this super-positioning of myth, art and language, that the wellspring of creativity flows.

The Surrealists, for their part, recognised the great power of these uncanny apparitions and dream-like sequences, referring to them in their notions of objective chance, yet this simply harkens back to an earlier esoteric tradition of alchemical knowledge, firmly embedded within disciplinary canon by the now apocryphal architectural allegory the *Hypnerotomachia Poliphili,* penned in the late 1400s by the mysterious Brother Colonna.[8] Navigating a poetically charged landscape filled with implausible architectural follies and phantasmagorical constructs, our eponymous hero finally discovers his beloved Polia (literally, many things, referring to architecture's inherent multiplicity) at the conjunction of logic and lust – the '*Vita Voluptuaria*',[9] a place where the fulfilment of desire is never fully present nor fully absent, manifesting instead as a paradoxically concurrent recollection and projectection, a mindfulness wholeness, and an awareness of otherness and ethical responsibility.

Imbued with emotive power, the dream-like sequences of images that comprise the phantasmagorical vision permit a fluidic mixing of remembered fragments and imagined figments, mediating impossible transpositions of the literal, metaphorical and allegorical meaning. Rendered soluble, the primordial constituents of reality meet in a condition of super-positioned syzygetic alignment, revealing spaces, places and technologies that have neither been previously witnessed nor wholly imagined.

Peter J Baldwin, *She comes, unbidden She comes,* 'Filigreed Gods – Diaphanous Bodies and Sacred Vessels', 2022

opposite right: Traversing the threshold of dreams and desires, considering the apparition of the phantom and the sensory confusion it generates; objects out of time, unearthly and beguiling forms, suggesting but not stating familiarity and recognisability.

are doorways to forbidden paths and the dark forest of desire

X-ray(t)ed Vision(s)

This inextricable link between the image and the imagination is not a new phenomenon; prior to German astronomer and mathematician Johannes Kepler's discovery of optics early in the 17th century,[10] both vision and conception were understood to operate as a form of projection[11] in which hidden 'virtual' (real but not actual) images – phantasma – function as intermediaries between the object of perception or conception and a receiving surface: the eye or the mind.

Not unlike the X-rays with which they are often conflated in psychoanalytical and artistic theory, the transformative effect of the phantom abolishes the traditional distinctions between interiority and exteriority. Just as the X-ray transforms the body, so too can the phantasm render the drawing a site of architectural experience, revealing the ephemeral traces and residues of construction, the multiplicity of architectural creation, and a subtle web of hidden structures and relational entanglements that make up the anteriority and interiority (described by Peter Eisenman as the 'diagram of architecture')[12] of the proposition, while at the same time projecting the more overt atmospherics of exteriority and spatial potential.

Reconceptualised in this way as a form of phantasmagorical projection, the drawing, no longer seen as a sterile and segregatory surface, becomes a threshold, an interface to a realm of architectural potential. Rejecting the confines of perspectival construction, the purpose is not to visualise space, but to evoke an 'atmosphere' redolent with notable characteristics of a space, place or programme alongside more esoteric information, permitting a promiscuous mixing of signs and signifiers while holding and sustaining these often-heterogeneous fragments on their own terms without the forfeiture of meaning that the reduction to a singular perspective so often brings.

Neither instantaneous nor autonomous, the practice of phantasmagorical drawing is intended to allow the architect (and the reader) to negotiate the complexities of tacit intuition and tangible constraint, shaping not only physical experience, but mediating intellectual, cultural and poetic connotations to invoke or perhaps provoke emotive response and imaginative engagement.

Love and Hunger

Poised on the cusp of representational artefact and spatial effect, my phantasmagorical drawings occupy this disruptive and generative interstitiality; they are the X-ray(t)ed thresholds of a realm of thickened and foliated surfaces, indeterminate dimensions and deep durations. Refuges for the uncertain and the numinous, the ephemeral traces that imbue our environments and by extension our architecture with meaning and emotive power. Composed as a series of dialectical dreamscapes, they are doorways to forbidden paths and the dark forest of desire.

Assembled from the fragments of history, myth and legend, from narrative and ritual, from architectural trope and artistic conceit, each drawing is a symbolically functioning proposition, a spectral tableau, which muses on the tragic consequences of postmodernism. Much like Dr Hoffman's great engines powered by the residues and excretions of his menagerie of lovers in their wire cages,[13] these constructs, these 'diaphanous bodies', are powered by a yearning for meaning for the lost, latent and poetic – the ephemeral otherness that was once fundamental to our world.

To view these drawings is to become embroiled in a foliated space of soluble signs, syncopated syzygetic alignments, and the random swerves of (objective) chance, allowing room for uncertainty and serendipitous emergence while inherently implicating the viewer in the construction of meaning and the act(ion) of mediation. Negotiating the threshold of exteriority and interiority, the tensional play of lust and logic allows them to be continuously reread. With each (re)reading, new meaning, and maybe more importantly, deeper understanding, can be found.

To read these drawings is to cross a threshold, to enter a world in which the synthetic projections of an epistemological construct are enacted on the surface of a pregnable membrane. They are the chromosomes of my dreams, the genetics of my desires choreographed by chance, change and serendipity poised on the moment of becoming. ∆

Notes

1. Angela Carter, *The Infernal Desire Machines of Dr Hoffman*, Rupert Hart Davis (London), 1974, p 244.
2. André Breton, *Manifestoes of Surrealism*, University of Michigan Press (Ann Arbour, MI), 1972, p 293.
3. Jean Baudrillard, 'Objects, Images, and the Possibilities of Aesthetic Illusion', in Nicholas Zurbrugg (ed), *Art and Artifact*, Sage Publications (London), 1997, p 12.
4. Jacques Derrida, *Positions*, University of Chicago Press (Chicago, IL), 1982.
5. Dalibor Vesely, *Architecture in the Age of Divided Representation*, MIT Press (Cambridge, MA), 2006, p 13.
6. 'Phantasm'; Merriam-Webster.com: www.merriam-webster.com/dictionary/phantasm.
7. Martin Heidegger, *On Time and Being*, Harper & Row (New York), 1972, p 69.
8. Francesco Colonna, *Hypnerotomachia Poliphili*, Thames & Hudson (London), 2005.
9. Alberto Pérez-Gómez, *Polyphilo*, MIT Press (Cambridge, MA), 1994, p XVII
10. Max Caspar, *Kepler*, Dover Publications (New York), 2003, p 142.
11. Tom Gunning, 'To Scan a Ghost: The Ontology of Mediated Vision', *Grey Room* 26, Winter 2007, pp 94–127.
12. Peter Eisenman, *Diagram Diaries*, Universe Press (New York), 1999, p 28.
13. Carter, *op cit*, p 261.

Text © 2024 John Wiley & Sons Ltd.
Images © Peter J Baldwin

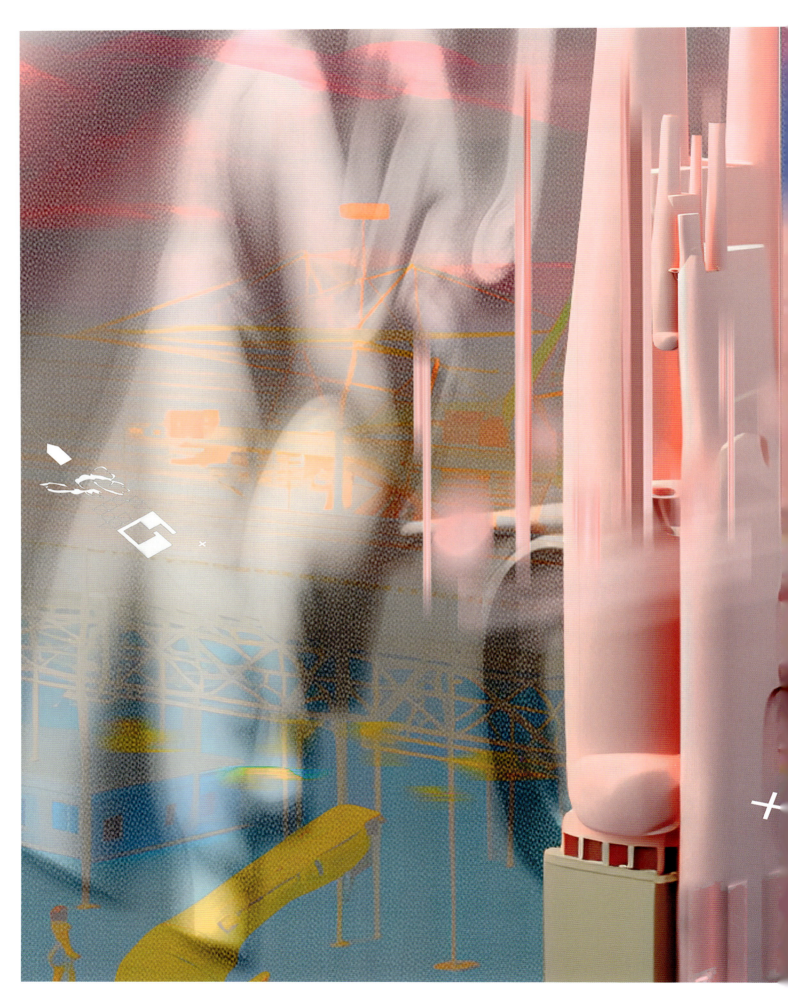

Perry Kulper

All Visualisations Have Crooked Tales/Tails

```
Perry Kulper and Eilís Finnegan,
Gifting, Ghosting & Gigabytes (detail),
Chicago Architecture Biennial,
Chicago Cultural Centre,
2023
```

The breadth of architectural typologies is waning, or so **Perry Kulper**, Professor of Architecture at Taubman College, University of Michigan, tells us. Kulper's work has for decades focused on the development of dexterous, agile and creative methodologies for speculating about the possibilities of architecture(s) explored through notions of equivalence, remixing, reinterpreting and reimagining. Developed through seven spatial spectral strategies for an installation at the 2023 Chicago Architecture Biennial, familiar landmarks of the city are rescaled and combined to become other implements, adornments and spaces, bringing an uncanny familiarity to their propositions.

Perry Kulper and Eilis Finnegan, *Gifting, Ghosting & Gigabytes,* Chicago Architecture Biennial, Chicago Cultural Centre, 2023

opposite left: Inspired by Baroque banquets and painted ceilings, a table-like construct was occupied by a collection of 3D-printed objects that refer to Chicago, to meals and to collective caring. It was paired with four panels, inspired by Hieronymus Bosch's painting *The Garden of Earthly Delights* (c 1500). This staged rehearsal told stories – all gifting, sometimes ghosting and always gigabyting.

Every traveller has a home of his own, and he learns to appreciate it the more from his wandering.
— Charles Dickens, 'Commercial Travellers', 1854[1]

Frequently motivated by systematic thinking, profit gains and intolerant time schedules, the production and implementation of architecture have given up the province of the latent world. Seldom do they take up the fertile promise of the flâneur or dérive – realms of driftings and wanderings. Rather, architecture's conceptions, production and materialisation amplify things that are measurable, quantifiable and normally driven by logic(s) and reason(s) that have expected and functionally motivated outcomes. This condition is demonstrated perhaps most explicitly by the dominance of reductive program(matic) typologies, often limiting the significance of architecture.

Engaging indeterminacy, uncertainty and latency allows a productive and disruptive reframing of architectures that have come to overly predict and prescribe our experiences. By establishing a sense of incompleteness, we can open creative and experiential opportunities that enable participation through acts of translation – a co-construction of experience that establishes relations between the sense of spatial settings and cultural belonging.

below right: A 'Hauntological Framework of Seven Spectral Strategies' – comprising Behind-the-Scenes; Margins and Peripheries; Traces; Language Folds and Speciated Programs; Analogic Thinking; Typological Rerouting; and Chimeras and Hybrids – was used to frame the research and provide a set of creative stimuli for the installation. Behind-the-Scenes tactics valued occupying literal and metaphorical rigs, jigs and moulds – revealing that which is normally tidied up and removed from sight. This Behind-the-Scenes view highlights a work in progress, indeterminate in its destinations – the laying of the table, plots, bioplastic prints and pesky pins.

Produced in collaboration with Eilís Finnegan, Assistant Professor of Environmental Design at Auburn University College of Architecture, Design and Construction in Auburn, Alabama, and first shown at the fifth Chicago Architecture Biennial (CAB 5) – titled 'This is a Rehearsal' – in the autumn of 2023, the speculative project *Gifting, Ghosting & Gigabytes* (referred to hereafter as *3Gs*) took flight into the skies of the Windy City, touching on latent, indeterminate and uncertain conditions.

3Gs visualised several strategically chosen urban rehearsals, represented and real, that referred to the Biennial's title. Partial in its articulation, rangy in its communicative ambitions and risky in its scope, it told stories using tone and character to establish a sense of familiar strangeness. The installation at CAB 5 invited a broad range of experiences by engaging things of historical and cultural import; the now and the then. The project challenged binary logics and tickled things just out of reach. It harvested behind-the-scenes processes and speciated aerial chimeras, rooftop hybrids and grounded misfits, to augment approaches to architecture based on reason, logic and instrumentality. It basked in heterogeneity by cross-splicing worlds and at times rerouting persistent disciplinary tropes like typologies, the form-follows-function paradigm and representational conventions.

Inviting an open-minded investigation and inquiry into peripheral conditions oft overlooked by the mainstream of the discipline, the work pointed to the indeterminate and unknown that might be discovered through broadened representational and spatial dexterities. It facilitated alternative ways for architects to operate below ordained disciplinary 'surfaces' – advantageous for architects who normalise experiences through the production of architecture. This approach foregrounded more fertile connections to existential, mysterious and uncertain terrains, gone missing in an age of logic and reason.

Motivated by generous gestures of listening, revealing and witnessing, *3Gs* ventured into upper atmospheres, rooftops and painted ceilings – real, fictional and abstract. Accomplished through scenographic settings and visual storytelling images, it choreographed requiems for the sky, prompting a rereading of embedded and latent spatial narratives that reinvigorated margins and peripheries – incomplete histories and the untold stories of the city that haunt our peripheral vision.

For our storytelling purposes we learned from the Surrealists

Operational Cartographies and Crooked Tales/Tails

To frame and explore the unknown conditions of Chicago for *3Gs*, a set of mythic probes were deployed. This 'Hauntological Framework of Seven Spectral Strategies' provided relational catalysts for spectral speciation. Strategies of varied capacities were leveraged – some as 'sites for work' for designers (Behind-the-Scenes; Margins and Peripheries; and Traces), others as operational allies (Language Folds and Speciated Programs; Analogic Thinking; and Typological Rerouting) and another acted as a design prompt and behavioural aspiration (Chimeras and Hybrids). All seven possessed qualities of ambiguity, slippage or uncertainty, relevant to the ambitions of *3Gs* and to the framing of this issue. These strategies paid homage to Wallace Stevens's poem *Thirteen Ways of Looking at a Blackbird* (1917),[2] which points to but never explicitly describes a blackbird – all the while drawing out other capacities of said bird. The poem's conceptual structure acted as a cartographical guide for the work, offering a promiscuous ballast for those of us tempted by the seduction of ghosted cosmologies.

Complementarily, tactics developed by Dadaist and Surrealist writers, painters and sculptors acted as relational shuttles to prompt these spectral strategies into action. Spirited by the manifestoes of André Breton, the work of French artists Marcel Duchamp and René Magritte, German artist Max Ernst and Spanish artist Salvador Dalí, the Surrealists awakened bourgeois culture from a state of malaise by stimulating the ghosts of the psychological interior – a treasure trove of hidden potential locked and ready to augment logic and reason by activating an alternative range of experiential frontiers. For our storytelling purposes we learned from the Surrealists. Akin to theirs, our tactics included the disruptive juxtaposition of Chicago landmarks with icons drawn from disparate scales and distant realities – William W Boyington's Chicago Water Tower (1869) with Rococo candlesticks, Ludwig Mies van der Rohe's IBM Plaza (1973) with cutlery holders, and Hammond, Beeby & Babka's Harold Washington Library Center (1991) with a napkin stand; paradoxical illusion – dining under Alexander Calder's *Flamingo* (1974) in Federal Plaza with tabletop traces of warped reflections, tattoos of memories made and critical fragments of plates for big proportions; and familiar strangeness – a gold-leafed version of Anish Kapoor's public sculpture *Cloud Gate* (2006), aka 'the Bean', in Millennium Park. These tactics were catalysts for slightly off-kilter experiences and harvesting things that had drifted, flâneur-like, just off the map.

The visualisations that accompany this article are manifestations of multiple and mutable combinations of the Seven Strategies. Their conceptual, diagrammatic and operational production utilised the generative AI program Midjourney; the 3D modelling software Blender; and the image creation, graphic design and photo editing software Photoshop. And like the storytelling visualisations, the software programs are harbingers for latent potential – in their own right. Crossbred, speciated and experimental, they had crooked tails and told crooked tales.

Perry Kulper and Eilís Finnegan,
Gifting, Ghosting & Gigabytes,
Chicago Architecture Biennial,
Chicago Cultural Centre,
2023

opposite left: The Traces spectral strategy has retentive and projective capacities. Here it is rendered as a storytelling scene for a post-Chicago Architecture Biennial party, tracing Chicago confetti, a meal setting, residues of occupation and temporal sleights of hand – dining under the flamingo with tabletop traces of worlds of warped reflections, tattoos of memories made and critical fragments of plates for big proportions.

opposite right: Language Folds and Speciated Programs augmented didactic, homogeneous frames of reference and explicit logics to engage the content of this work more effectively. Here, a reimagined structure from the Chicago World's Fair of 1893 facilitates aerial rooftop gardens for Arduinos, atmospheric stockyards for airships, and steel structures for seasonal celebrations. This world is curious about the Chicago City Hall Rooftop Garden (2000), the ill-fated experimental *Wingfoot* Air Express (1919) and ghost stories from the skyline.

above: Analogic Thinking enables designers to work through likenesses, referring to things, conceptual frameworks and qualities outside of their own authorial capacities. This table plan learned, analogously, from Baroque ceiling storytelling and Hieronymus Bosch's *The Garden of Earthly Delights* (c 1500). to organise table settings and coordinate courses, whilst ambience-inducing hybrids like the Chicago Water Tower with a Rococo candlestick, the IBM Plaza with a cutlery holder and the Harold Washington Library Center with a napkin stand paraded about.

97

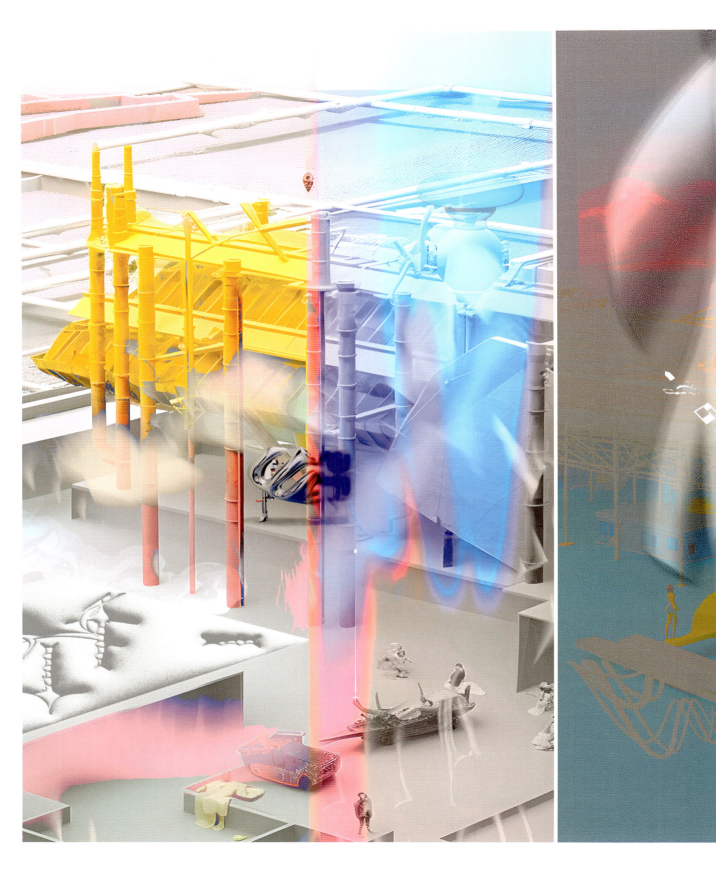

Collective Care

Arguably, contemporary spatial and representational conversations must navigate a multitude of ambiguous worlds – a result of global entanglements linked to ideological, political, economic and practised conditions. An outcome of the abandonment of collective caring. These negotiations are essential, critical in fact, if architecture is to make a difference. This is particularly important as architecture has largely been stripped of its shared forms of communication, cultural literacy and agency. Engaging indeterminacy, latency and uncertainty – linked to forms of ambiguity – provides opportunities for igniting the greatest conceptual, physical, psychological and emotional depths of human and nonhuman entities, by harvesting less explicit relations and increasing the potential to experience the world in fuller dimensions.

The Spectral Strategies served as the deeper structuring for the three themes that framed *3Gs*. Gifting was rehearsed through multiple forms of host generosity, overstaying and underdressing our welcome and giving back to Chicago; Ghosting found, remembered and translated forgotten histories (steam plant, shipyard and shipwreck pasts), evacuated events (the rebirth of World's Fair fleets, Chicago confetti and seasonal celebrations) and the invisibility of constraints in aerial territories (atmospheric stockyards for airships); and Gigabytes rumbled round pixelated skies, sky-decked datasets and file hijacking.

Visual storytelling in the project was situated in relation to the emergence of 'design fiction', a term articulated by Bruce Sterling in 2005.[3] Frequently design fiction relates to background signals in our experiences like innovative technologies and emergent cultural phenomena – using those encounters to reroute societal patterns and expectations about the world. In parallel it is related to the narrative turn which is characterised by using narrative constructions to give meaning, or significance, to something. In *3Gs* the visual stories told foregrounded the possibility for shared communication across multiple publics.

Perry Kulper and Eilis Finnegan,
Gifting, Ghosting & Gigabytes,
Chicago Architecture Biennial,
Chicago Cultural Centre,
2023

opposite: The Margins and Peripheries spectral strategy cared for conditions orphaned and out of sight. This experimental view hosted mechanical systems redefining their roles, gigabytes hitching rides, and scores in snowdrifts. It was curious about ghosts of steam-plant pasts, shipyards and shipwrecks, the Fisk Generating Station, the 104th Street dry docks and industrial air rights. Cranes craned for better views.

left: The tactic of Typological Rerouting suggested that the long-held disciplinary bearing of typologies is on the wane. As complicated world algorithms unfold, typologies might be inadequate to the task of positively harvesting the entanglements of globalised practices. This modelled exploration learned from Chicago's elevated 'L'-train tracks, trusses and bridge-tending houses for restructuring the city's riversides – referring to programmes like the Jackson Street Bridge Tender's House and the old Lake Street Bridge over the Chicago River (both 1916).

Perry Kulper and Eilís Finnegan,
Gifting, Ghosting & Gigabytes,
Chicago Architecture Biennial,
Chicago Cultural Centre,
2023
Chimeras and Hybrids are crossbreeds that challenged the dominance of static, 'forever' architecture. Dynamic and temporally adept species, they choreographed nuanced or sudden spatial and programmatic emphases, transforming and motivating environments. This experimental image engaged with a roofscape via AI-generated states, suspecting phases of the rebirth of former World's Fair fleets, Louis Sullivan dupes and neo-Gothic in neon.

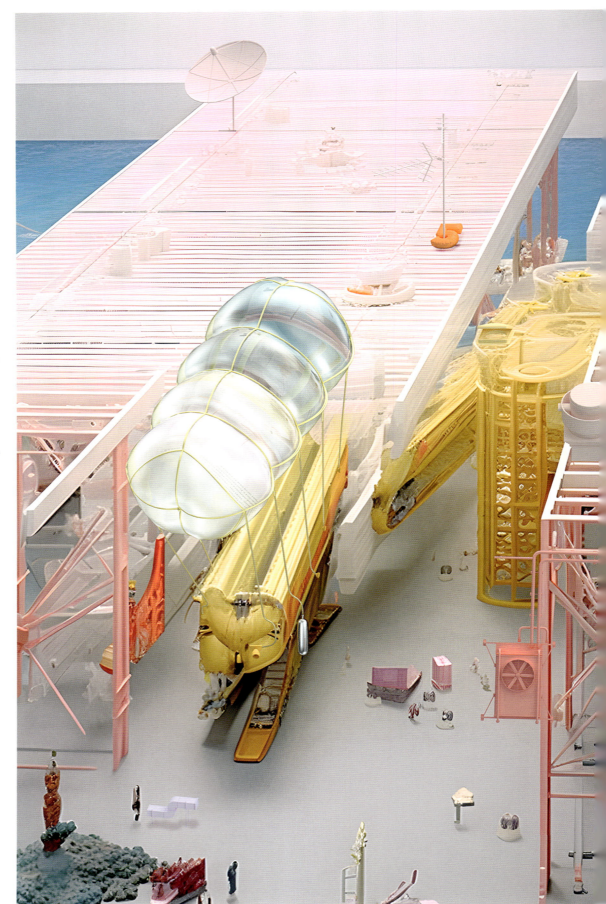

100

For the installation, a table-like construct hosted a diverse array of guests. A literal and metaphorical gathering device inspired by Baroque banquets, painted ceilings and collective assembly tables, it was occupied by an eclectic entourage of 3D-printed totemic elements – a salt-and-pepper-shaker 'building', a library becoming a napkin holder, and a water tower becoming a candlestick. Each referring to Chicago, to meals, to collective generosity and to forms of shared communication. To collective caring. The table was paired with four vertical and digital print-bedecked panels inspired by the Netherlandish painter Hieronymus Bosch's *The Garden of Earthly Delights* (*c* 1500) and its narrative capacities, topical range and cultural reach. The panels and table staged explicit and implicit forms of communication, set in the guise of delectable rehearsals, of all kinds, shapes and sizes … telling stories, all gifting, occasionally ghosting and always gigabyting.

Heterogeneous interests and tactics for *3Gs* included engagements with global and situated aerial realms; (a/un/non/multi-)scalar shenanigans, shifts and slippages; a(erial)-gravitational spacescapes; light speed, Mach speed, computational speeds and no speeds; optical seductions and visual presents/presence; deep mythologies and historically rich evidentiary fields; buoyant skies, aerial tolls, air rights and write-offs; rooftops, drones, Arduinos and all manner of buoyant transport; aerial acrobats, highwire acts and sleight-of-hand cloud(ed) storytellers; fakes, dupes, dumps and dropouts; remote access and virtual private networks (VPNs); nonbinary worlds – chimeras, hybrids and things longing to become other; human and nonhuman transactional mischief; and a tensional play between the virtues of representation and the so-called real world. Ghosting(s), of all kinds, lurked nearby.

Promiscuous forms of representation and visualisations played significant roles in envisioning the proposal. As diffusion models, generative AI platforms and other digital formats implicate our lives at breakneck speed, *3Gs* indulged in some of them to explore operational dexterity, design versatility and disciplinary expansions necessary for these contemporary architects. The digitally generated species leveraged scenography, myriad infrastructural and operational systems, aspects of project management, archaeology, cultural history, graphic design, literary references and varied spatial practices. Prompted rehearsals of AI contributed to ongoing pedagogical and think-tank debates and practices linked to questions of authorship and authenticity while structuring work that tickled hidden Chicago and the domains of data centres, their airspace, digital debris, e-waste and computational literacy.

Other Frontiers
Without question, emerging global frontiers – new wildernesses – demand the architect to be many architects. Linked forever to the worlds of indeterminacy, latency and the unknowable, to AI and to unpredictable futures, we might even need to morph into ghostly/ghosted/ghosting storytellers. Becoming other … chimeras, hybrids. All of us. The alarms are ringing and the smoke detectors raging as we venture into alternative frontiers filled with ambiguous entanglements, inexplicable algorithms and the pleasures of indulging in that which evades us – dancing with new mythologies, alternative gods, unsung heroes and normal everyday folk(lore) – the affordances of worlds, lying in the shadows, dormant, but ready for activation to make deep contributions to our experiences. Waiting.

In *3Gs*, seven spectral strategies (of which there are many more) mixed with Surrealist-inspired tactics exposed new 'sites of work' for these architects – for the construction of alternative stories, towards forms of generosity and collective care. Gifting. Historically, mythologies have allowed cultures to touch and at times explain the latent world. Perhaps now, the work of representation – who is represented (enlarged publics) and what is represented (in our case using generative AI, digital modelling and image effects) might allow architects the means to navigate the emerging potential of these new entanglements, new wildernesses. Latent worlds. Ghosting. Gifting & Ghosting, coupled with the virtues of all forms of digitality, that are immanently harvestable, lurking. Gigabyting.

The world is a machine-learned oyster, with its feet on the ground and its heads, so many, in the sky. As true cultural agents, it is up to architects, becoming other, to invent the algorithms, operational protocols and representational and material instantiations to reveal the capacities of those metaphorical pearls. To excel in these new horizons, the architect must be many architects. Dexterous, versatile and transformable.

Perhaps the last word should be given to Alice, with Charles Dickens, author of many a ghostly tale himself, riding shotgun:

> It's no use going back to yesterday, because I was a different person then.
> — Lewis Carroll, *Alice's Adventures in Wonderland*, 1865[4]

Crooked tails begetting crooked tales …

Notes
1. Charles Dickens, 'Commercial Travellers', speech given at the Anniversary Dinner in commemoration of the foundation of the Commercial Travellers' Schools, held at the London Tavern, 30 December 1854: www.classicbookshelf.com/library/charles_dickens/speeches_literary_and_social/13/.
2. Wallace Stevens, *13 Ways of Looking at a Blackbird*, Stephen F Austin State University Press (Nacogdoches, TX), 2013.
3. Bruce Sterling, *Shaping Things*, MIT Press (Cambridge, MA), 2005.
4. Lewis Carroll, *Alice's Adventures in Wonderland*, T.Y. Crowell & Co, New York and Boston, 1893, p 125.

Text © 2024 John Wiley & Sons Ltd. Images: pp 92–3, 96–100 © Perry Kulper. AI-generated images created in Midjourney using /blend; p 95 © Perry Kulper

Night Kitchen,
Beneath the Glitter,
2024

left: Night Kitchen confronts the mundane with the magical, reimagining the domestic and realities that coexist. Images such as this will often be developed within book layouts placed in further exploratory imagery, in an uncertain intertwining of fact and fiction.

opposite: Night Kitchen write, design and illustrate publications that can only be found within the worlds communicated by their imagery. Intermingled with such approaches will often be visual citations to wider academic influences.

Ifigeneia Liangi and Daniel Dream

A TAILORED REALITY INSIDE IN HERE

Night Kitchen,
Excerpt of a Working Process,
2023
Night Kitchen often explores the design process itself within the development of narratives. The initial notes and studies for this scene are included here as a part of the image they contributed to, with the image becoming an artefact haunted by its own process.

Publishing, a discipline which encompasses the creation of both the content and form of a book, has played a central role in the development of architectural practice as we know it today. From antiquity, through the strange awakenings of the Renaissance and the innovations of the 20th century, the framing of books as generators of discourse has been integral to a version of the discipline in which architects conceive ideas about architecture alongside architectural designs.[1] Night Kitchen is a practice that actively explores the production of books, particularly picturebooks, which are guided by postmodern spatial logics, made possible by the format's interplay of verbal and visual components – a condition that has intriguing implications for architectural imagery when utilised as a means of disseminating designs.

Conceived as a design research practice with dual home-studios in London and Athens, Night Kitchen defies conventional boundaries, encompassing architectural designing, publishing and collecting. Its studios serve as domestic-office archives housing repositories of found artefacts and popular cultural ephemera. Established to explore the creative potential of the supposed gaps between binary understandings of fact and fiction, framed through the lens of imaginary picturebooks that both display and are displayed within the studio's speculative imagery, the work produced by Night Kitchen blends the tangible reality of the real world with the fantastical realms of fiction, in order to explore the indeterminate exchanges that occur between narrative realms, designing and making. The incorporation of items acquired from other fictional worlds and related spheres, including screen-used cinematic props and the personal belongings of key inspirational figures, adds a hauntological layer to this practice, with this approach to design exploration allowing for stories and fabrications to be imbued with elements from the cultural past, giving agency and value to the opaque relationships between the real and the imagined. These objects are incorporated into the act of storytelling, folded into the development of design and the production of words and images. The resultant imagery is often saturated with wider narratives and indeterminate relationships, acting as a mediating link between the mundanity of the studio space and more mythical realms.

These tales serve as repositories in a way that mirrors the cluttered spaces in which they are conceived, the picturebook being used as a site for the past to latently intermingle with the

Operating from dual locations in London and Athens, the output of Night Kitchen, the experimental architectural research lab of **Ifigeneia Liangi and Daniel Dream**, often takes the form of anarchitectural story books, illustrated with congested, postmodern interiors full of colourful objects and artefacts. But these are not random juxtapositions of stuff – they are elaborate, multilayered tableaux, their cross-currents haunted with associations that stretch far and wide across film, sport, literature, memorabilia, art practice and time.

present, and for the real to overlap with the imagined. In doing so, the format emerges as an unexpected medium for exploring the implicit possibilities and spectral interplays of design representation. Key to this is a fluid mixing of the verbal and the visual, the spatial and the temporal, objects and images, and the magical and the practical, with this interweaving taking place in the gaps usually expected to sit between these criteria, engaging architecture not just as a collection of physical elements, but as an uncertain cache of histories and resonances. A key element of the studio's work are considerations on the significance of publishing for the history of architectural practice, and the implications of engaging in the production of a different kind of book in connection with the specifics of a different kind of practice.

Reading Space: The Bookishness of Books
The popularity of picturebooks gradually grew during the 20th century, with the format being defined by its interconnected visual and textual narratives. Notable figures in this history include Beatrix Potter, Dr Seuss and Maurice Sendak, illustrator-authors whose work is likely to be familiar to any former child. According to Sendak, whose publications – most famously *Where the Wild Things Are* (1963)[2] – have since been studied extensively, the perception of these books as being for children resulted in their being undervalued as an art form. Consequently, the format was pigeonholed into the nursery until scholarship in the 1970s and 1980s began to take their peculiarities as a focus of serious enquiry,[3] with key figures such as Perry Nodelman asking 'what happened when words accompanied pictures and pictures accompanied words'.[4] An established literary scholar, Nodelman found himself perplexed when attempting to describe the interactions within the picturebooks he encountered after being tasked with teaching a children's literature course. The deeper Nodelman delved into the subject, the more he observed unique relationships between words and images. In contrast to traditional illustrated tales, the imagery in picturebooks is not 'solely at the service of the image'.[5] Instead, the images convey something that words alone cannot communicate in the development of a narrative. The particularity of these relationships led Nodelman to conclude that picturebooks encourage a unique form of thinking.[6] Noted scholar Barbara Bader recognised the format's value as hinging on the limitless potential within its interrelated yet simultaneously independent words and images.[7]

'the words tell us what the pictures do not show, and the pictures show us what the words do not tell us'

· Chapter 1 / Solid Tinsel _ p.26 ·

The Arrival of the Fourth and Fifth Dimensions
Since the work of Bader and Nodelman, the interplays central to picturebooks have evolved, becoming more complex. Of particular interest is the influence of postmodernism on the peritextual, intertextual and spatial possibilities that arise from the nonstandard layouts and picturebook-specific spatial strategies which have been used to enable interplays between fictional and real space. Traditionally picturebooks relied on an approach where, as Lawrence R Sipe and Sylvia Pantaleo write in their book *Postmodern Picturebooks* (2016), 'the words tell us what the pictures do not show, and the pictures show us what the words do not tell us',[8] the images and text occupying separate realms on the page, and this is often still the case. This graphic segregation can also be observed, albeit differently, in the standardised format of contemporary architectural publications, which are indebted to the conventions of early European book culture, when a book's content was prioritised over its physical form.[9] However, in postmodern picturebooks, the realms of text, image and reader often meet in the margins and the in-between spaces of the layout, courtesy of a format-specific conception of the fourth dimension – described by Bradin Cormack and Carla Mazzio, Professors of English at the University of Chicago, as 'the (liminal/marginal) space shared between the image and the audience' – and a fifth dimension – 'a spatial area that exists beneath the physical page of the book'.[10] The words that you, the reader, are reading right now have a direct material relationship with these realms.

Night Kitchen develop fictional publications which can only be found in the imagery that accompanies their academic writing. Examples such as *Solid Tinsel* and *Zero Carbon Judy Garland* (both 2023) explore the spatial logics at play in recent picturebook scholarship while rethinking the conventions of the domestic architectural project, developing an alternative approach in which the act of designing and the generation of architectural elements produce a form of content, with the layout and sequencing of these fictional books being an extended spatial concern to the spaces they appear within.

Aspects of this extend what artist and architect Marian Macken has described as architecture's 'entwined relationship between the physicality of built work and the immaterial'.[11] An incorporation of the fourth and fifth dimensions explores depictions of the printed format as a mediating link between different realities. They allow textual and visual characters, and objects, to bleed between realms. Aspects of images sometimes transgress the frames they would traditionally be expected to reside in, being allowed to step out of a standardised page space and into a realm halfway between the story that constitutes their world and the book that contains them within ours. Whether in books or through the depiction of books, Night Kitchen's designs complicate various boundaries as part of the wild rumpus of the in-between, signalling a multiplicity of readings and meanings. They carry realities between realities, stories within stories, and issues of △ across issues of △.

Night Kitchen,
Beneath the Glitter,
2024
opposite: Night Kitchen's reimagining of their studio environment serves as the backdrop for the development of their narratives. By way of making a direct appearance as characters, the designers themselves frequently become integral elements of these stories.

Night Kitchen,
Zero Carbon Judy Garland,
2023
above: Images and spaces act as repositories for various narratives and worlds. Here, a telegram to Judy Garland appears next to mail received in Scene 90 of *Creed III* (2023), intertwined with the development of a layout.

Fantasies Grounded 10 Feet Deep in Reality

Such work draws attention to its fictitious nature, and its own picturebookishness, through further strategies, with imagery often making intertextual efforts to make spectral allusions to the work of others through an appropriation of places and elements from different tales. Also brought in are real-world objects acquired from other factual and fictional situations: the yellow cup and blue-green saucer that can be seen in *Solid Tinsel* were obtained from the café used for the filming of Jean-Pierre Jeunet's film *Amélie*,[12] with the copy of *The Method of Henry James* that appears nearby[13] having been bought at auction from the collection of Maurice Sendak's personal library – its pages releasing the smell of his smoking habit when opened and referred to, the olfactory shadow and spectral visitation of a primary source of inspiration.

Contained within an as-yet-unpublished manuscript titled 'The Available Stock of Reality: A Vade Mecum', intended to be developed in the imagery of future design research, is a catalogue of the various memorabilia that is gradually filling these studios – acquired through hours, months and years on various auction sites. A fascination with letters and notes has given rise to something of an unusual epistolary – a reverie of intercepted correspondence and handwritten missives that embraces the written word of both real and fictional characters. Displayed on a wall, an 1860 letter from the sculptor Félicie de Fauveau resides alongside a collection of handwritten letters sent by Muhammad Ali. A note from Janet Jackson can be found next to doodles by Maurice Sendak. The letters received by Adonis in a pivotal moment of *Creed III* (2023)[14] are stored beside a cheque signed by the Tin Man from Oz.[15] This collection resides at the confluence of fact and fiction, where the artefacts of actual individuals and events hold equal value to items from cinematic franchises.

Recent reappraisals of collecting as an art form have identified the practice as a complex realm of research, care and preservation.[16] It has also been seen as an act of 'world-acquisition' with the philosopher Norbert Hinske describing this as *Weltaneignung*, which can be understood as meaning to allow oneself to be enchanted by the world.[17] Unlike traditional

collectors, who procure rather than create, Night Kitchen's approach differs. Objects are acquired for the sake of a creative integration, and are placed within the work as catalysts for the development of ideas and narratives, while hinting at unspoken connections, as an agency to explore myth, story and the imagined. As such, the studio's drawings and books serve as hauntological repositories for other fictions in a way that echoes the space these narratives are developed in. For those who see them, these elements bring the fictionality of the work to the forefront. Through this inclusion of real-world objects which encapsulate wider narratives, and the way the studio's rethinking of the domestic plays within and around the liminal spaces of their chosen format, Night Kitchen's twofold approach aims to narrow the gap between history, other fictions and the reader, as a critical exploration of where fact and fiction are expected to sit in relation to one another. The studio's work holds the traces of multiple moments, as further games take place in the fourth and fifth dimensions – this is a practice where being pushed into the margins might be no bad thing. ∆

Notes
1. See Mike Aling, 'Publishing as Architectural Practice', *Design Ecologies* 6 (1), 2017, p 86.
2. Maurice Sendak, *Where the Wild Things Are*, Harper & Rowe (New York), 1963.
3. See for example Salman Rushdie, *The Wizard of Oz*, BFI Publishing (London), 1992, p 18.
4. Perry Nodelman, 'Introduction', in Naomi Hamer, Perry Nodelman and Mavis Reimer (eds), *More Words about Pictures*, Routledge (London), 2017, p 1.
5. Torsten Schmiedeknecht, Jill Rudd and Emma Hayward (eds), *Building Children's Worlds: The Representation of Architecture and Modernity in Picturebooks*, Routledge (London), 2023, p 3.
6. Nodelman, *op cit*, p 3.
7. Barbara Bader, *American Picturebooks from Noah's Ark to the Beast Within*, Macmillan (London), 1977, p 8.
8. Lawrence R Sipe and Sylvia Pantaleo (eds), *Postmodern Picturebooks: Play, Parody, and Self-Referentiality*, Routledge (London), 2016, p 9.
9. See Bradin Cormack and Carla Mazzio, *Book Use, Book Theory: 1500–1700*, University of Chicago Press (Chicago,IL), 2005, p 2.
10. *Ibid*.
11. Marian Macken, *Binding Space: The Book as Spatial Practice*, Routledge (London), 2018, p 25.
12. Jean-Pierre Jeunet (director), *Amélie*, Claudie Ossard Productions, 2001.
13. Joseph Warren Beach, *The Method of Henry James*, Yale University Press (New Haven, CT), 1918.
14. Michael B Jordan (director), *Creed III*, Chartoff-Winkler Productions and Metro-Goldwyn-Mayer, 2023.
15. Jack Haley, the actor who played the Tin Man in Victor Fleming (director), *The Wizard of Oz*, Metro-Goldwyn-Mayer, 1939.
16. See Kevin Melchionne, 'Collecting as an Art' in *Philosophy and Literature* 23 (1), 1999, pp 148–56.
17. *Ibid*, p 151.

Night Kitchen,
Solid Tinsel,
2023
opposite left: Turning the page to reveal a fifth dimension, the elements of other tales appear in an image alongside a book on the novelist Henry James once owned and referred to by author-illustrator Maurice Sendak in the development of his own work. Sendak is often considered to be the 20th century's most seminal picturebook artist.

Night Kitchen,
Fictional picturebook for a fictional picturebook,
2023
opposite right: A spread from *The Right Side of Paradise*, an imagined work of fiction that regularly appears in imagery created to complement the studio's academic writings. A spread from *Beneath the Glitter*, a similar fictional title, can be seen in the reflection of the book stand's mirror.

Night Kitchen,
Zero Carbon Judy Garland,
2024
left: 'Just Landed', a frontispiece for one of the fictional books the studio have developed as a part of their design research. Here, a domestic scene is utilised for the placement of peritext.

Text © 2024 John Wiley & Sons Ltd.
Images © Night Kitchen

Mike Phillips

Mike Phillips, *After the Flammarion*, 2023
This image pays homage to a wood engraving from Camille Flammarion's book *L'atmosphère: météorologie populaire*, published in 1888. *After the Flammarion* extends the dimensions beyond the engraving's celestial dome, adding another layer to the material and immaterial universe, to capture emerging contemporary algorithmic entities and digital ectoplasm.

Michael Powell and Emeric
Pressburger (directors),
A Matter of Life and Death,
Eagle-Lion Films,
1946
Dr Frank Reeves, played by the actor Roger Livesey, speaks for the defence in one of the film's celestial court sequences. He argues that the love between Squadron Leader Peter Carter, played by the actor David Niven, and radio operator June, played by Kim Hunter, is more powerful than Heaven's accounting bureaucracy, after Peter misses his prescribed date with death.

'This is the Universe, big isn't it.' It has got considerably bigger since British actor John Longden's calming narration of the opening sequence of the 1946 film *A Matter of Life and Death*.[1] He introduces us to a cosmic transscalar shift, a slow zoom from the depths of space to focus on the trauma of war on planet Earth. This transition from the meta to the meso scale is familiar filmic trope, such as the closing credit sequence of the 'Supermarionation' television series *Fireball XL5* (1962)[2] and *Star Trek* film (2009),[3] and down to the micro scale with the short science documentary film *Powers of Ten* (1977) by Charles and Ray Eames.[4] However, this easy movement and flow through space, from planet to planet and galaxy to galaxy, travelling at impossible speeds over unimaginable distances, is always at a distance from the viewer via the flat TV or cinema screen: the vision of the infinite is severed by the rectangular edge. Immersion in infinity has always been the modus operandi of the cosmological architecture of the planetarium, and specifically the hemispherical screen of the fulldome. The fulldome surrounds the viewer, immersing them in the struggle to contain the ever-expanding observable universe in a dome-shaped box, some 46.5 billion light years out (and back in time) to its edge, requiring a collective metacognitive dissonance and consensual hallucination to appreciate how something so big can fit into something so small.

Suggesting a curious comparison between the Victorian séance and the contemporary world of immersive virtual environments, **Mike Phillips**, Professor of Interdisciplinary Arts at the University of Plymouth, and Director of Research at i-DAT.org, describes the new capabilities of the fulldome, which uses notions of the automatic movements of the planchette, the wooden token that traverses the alphanumeric surface of the notorious Ouija board, as a model for the development of a quasi-participatory audience interface he dubs the 'phage'. Clusters of phage can be manipulated by the viewer-occupiers of the dome to instigate all manner of formal, scalar and conceptual transpositionings.

Heavenly Architecture

The history of the fulldome is intertwingled with architectural mechanisms for viewing and representing the heavens, weaving the mythological, the divine and theological, the astronomical and astrological into the fabric of dome-shaped buildings that symbolise enlightenment. There are strangely compelling acoustic and visual properties of a dome, from the whispering-gallery effect to its ability to disappear completely when gazed into. When projected into, these qualities provide an enhanced sense of immersion, especially when the projection extends through the screen into the void beyond. It is in this space that collective consensual hallucinations exist – a space not dissimilar to the black and white architecture of heaven as portrayed in *A Matter of Life and Death*, with its celestial escalator, Records Office and Courtroom.

Spherical perspective is key to the physical architecture of the fulldome. It is core to the way we visually experience the world, and yet for some reason the flat image has dominated our culture. The eye is a sphere, we see through dome-shaped images falling on our retina, the sky is a dome, and we live on a spherical planet. The relationship between the eye, the projected image and the screen of the dome is cyclical and intimately linked.

In the film's opening zoom sequence, as we descend through the clouds and fog, we also get a sense of another dimension that is increasingly becoming a vital fabric of the fulldome: the Hertzian, the 'noises in the air'. Named after Heinrich Hertz, the German physicist who developed instruments to detect and manipulate electromagnetic waves, the Hertzian domain was a discovery that led to a blossoming of experimentation at the end of the 19th century – experiments that often blurred the boundaries between science and the occult and revealed a landscape as invisible as the celestial dimension, shifting the focus from an ocular truth to one which senses the world through lensless eyes.

The lens was always a problem for the contemporary fulldome content maker. To capture a spherical world a fish-eye lens was required, but then the circular image fell onto a rectangular image sensor or film, reducing the resolution by around a third. Where every pixel counts on the projected image, lens-captured content required complex compositing and stitching to retain fidelity. Whilst modern 360-degree cameras make video production a little easier, a culture of animation, digital 3D modelling and game engines has thrived, enabling a natural adoption of alternative sensing technologies. The Hertzian world is now captured through light detection and ranging (LiDAR), magnetic resonance imaging (MRI), atomic force microscopy (AFM) and real-time data feeds; essentially any form of computational media can be re-rendered within a spherical projection from meta, meso and micro scales. These instruments that do our seeing for us translate their digital hallucinations through data, and consequently the fulldome is less of a planetarium and more of an omniarium, a place where disciplines blend and provoke each other.

Anon,
The Flammarion engraving, in
Camille Flammarion's *L'atmosphère:
météorologie populaire*,
Librairie Hachette (Paris),
1888
below: The Flammarion print is a wood engraving by an unknown artist included in Camille Flammarion's book. It portrays a figure peeling back the canopy of the heavens at the point where the sky and earth meet and peeping out of their terrestrial confines into the celestial space beyond the heavens.

Looking back 100 years to the birth of the modern planetarium in the form of the Zeiss Planetarium in the Deutsches Museum, Munich, in 1923, the shift in perspective, from Earth to the heavens, was mirrored elsewhere by engineers, scientists and an eager public's desire to explore these parallel dimensions, in particular the Hertzian dimension. My *After the Flammarion* (2023) pays homage to the wood engraving printed in the French astronomer and author Camille Flammarion's book *L'atmosphere: météorologie populaire* (1888).[5] The unknown artist who made the engraving captures a blend of scientific wonder and celestial awe as the figure breaks through the dome and into the dimensions beyond. *After the Flammarion* montages the Screenberry calibration screen,[6] a media server used to map fulldomes for real-time playback, with the Zeiss-Kleinplanetarium No 1 (ZKP 1) Star Ball, an optical-mechanical constellation projection system, adding another dimension to the original Flammarion, somewhere beyond the astronomical and the Hertzian – a contemporary digital dimension where the flow of algorithmic entities can emerge. The incorporation of predictive and playful algorithms, interactive devices and real-time remote-sensing feeds transforms the fulldome into a new form of psychometric architecture.

As a definition of psychometrics, Robert L Morris, former Koestler Chair of Parapsychology at the University of Edinburgh, writes: 'The concept of objects (or places) seeming to record

Mike Phillips,
The Thanatorium - Looking Through Sol's Eyes,
2023
right: A reconstruction of the Thanatorium scene from the 1973 film *Soylent Green* as Sol departs – a translation from the original Cinerama space to a fulldome. The last image seen by Sol Roth, played by Edward G Robinson, was reconstructed, projected in the fulldome and photographed with a 360-degree camera, and here displayed in Tiny Planet mode. The retinas were added in post-production.

Mike Phillips,
Inside-Outside / Magnetic Resonance Imaging (MRI) to Volumetric Performative,
2023
opposite: The construction of a volumetric performative fulldome space. The image transitions (left to right) from MRI scans through to a volumetric model, and ends with the immersive fulldome projection.

events and then play them back for sensitive people is generally referred to as psychometry. The objects can be called psychometric objects or token objects.'[7] In a post-ocular world, where the eyes, once the windows to the soul, are replaced by sensing technologies and algorithmic processes that do our seeing for us, psychometry has the potential to replace traditional media experiences where our perspective on the 'real world' is increasingly understood through data and through things that are measured and felt rather than seen. The fulldome is an immersive architecture where all these different kinds of truth can seamlessly blend together.

But still there is awe and euphoria; immersion demands it and the artificial does not diminish it. Even in anticipation of our predicted death, the beauty of the profundity of tulips, in the immersive Thanatorium experience of the film *Soylent Green* (1973),[8] we are euphoric. In the dystopian world of New York City in 2022 a large-scale cinematic experience is the place to die. Filmed in a Cinerama, the scene is reconstructed in *The Thanatorium – Looking Through Sol's Eyes* (2023) as a 360-degree near-death experience in the open research lab i-DAT's Immersive Vision Theatre.[9] The Thanatorium is an architecture for death, a home for Thanatos the Greek god of death, and a place for euthanasia – a good (*eu*) death (*Thanatos*). The temporary conversion of an omniarium into a thanatorium gave a glimpse of the space beyond the fulldome as a performative dome-shaped death.

Data Apparitions

The construction of Munich's Zeiss Planetarium coincided with an international flurry of paranormal explorations of the Hertzian dimension, with the development of psychometric objects designed to communicate with the dead. For example, around the same time in the US, the inventor and entrepreneur Thomas Edison was building 'an apparatus to see if it is possible for personalities which have left this earth to communicate with us'.[10]

In 1930s Austria, Professor Gustav Adolf Schwaiger, technical director of the Österreichischer Rundfunk (ORF), the Austrian national broadcasting corporation, was constructing Hertzian instruments to explore the ectoplasm that would exude from infamous medium Rudi Schneider. I have made attempts to recover traces of their interactions from the atomic forces locked in a grain of dust obtained from the studio of an unknown female painter where their experiments were conducted. The 'Spectre' exhibition (2012) and ongoing fulldome work explores the possibility that the memories of these psychic-technologists were trapped in the detritus of the building, waiting to be unlocked with an atomic force microscope and an interactive assemblage and rendered as fleeting audio/visual ectoplasm from the unholy trinity.[11]

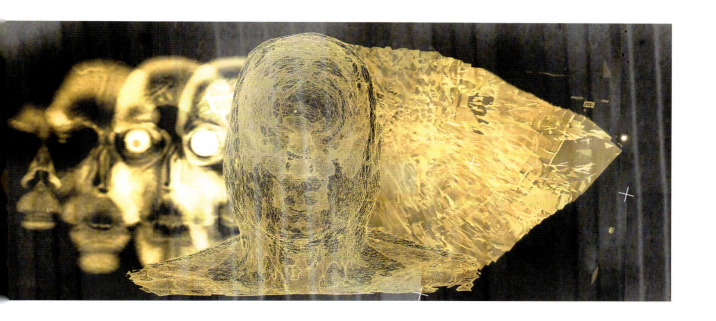

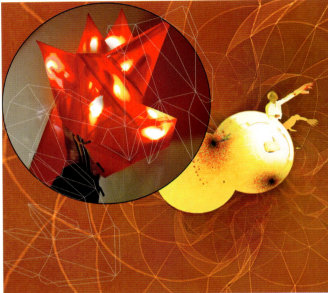

Mike Phillips,
The Phage,
2023
above left: Reworked montage of images captured from the E/M/D/L – European Mobile Dome Lab *Murmuration* performances from 2015 at the Society for Arts and Technology in Montreal, incorporating newly constructed AI-generated artefacts and audience members using phage – collaborative physical instruments that enable the manipulation of virtual objects.

Mike Phillips,
Phage Breaching the Fulldome Membrane,
2023
above right: Representing a fulldome on a two-dimensional plane can never do it justice: all sense of immersion and the transscalar is lost. This inverted 360-degree or 'tiny-planet' photograph shows a phage summoning AI-generated ectoplasm and includes an inset photograph of a 2023 version of a phage with biometric sensors.

Mike Phillips,
Phage Conjuring Ectoplasm,
2023
opposite: This tiny-planet photograph captures the AI-generated digital ectoplasm filling open research lab i-DAT's Immersive Vision Theatre fulldome.

Invoking digital ectoplasm in the fulldome, the E/M/D/L – European Mobile Dome Lab for artistic research (2013–15), an international, interdisciplinary collaboration, culminated in public fulldome performances at the Society for Arts and Technology, Montreal: *Liminal Spaces* (2015), *Dream Collider* (2015) and *Murmuration* (2015).[12] The works represented a synthesis of research undertaken into the fulldome as a shared virtual reality and a multidimensional transscalar space haunted by data apparitions recovered from the edge of the known universe and the depths of the nanosphere. *Murmuration* constructed a series of transscalar recursive transitions from volumetric AFM and MRI scans, rendered in 3D with a low polygon mesh aesthetic, to create the immersive environment. Aspects of this process are shown in the image *Inside–Outside* (2023).

Audiences could navigate the fulldome virtual spaces through playful interaction with algorithmic particle swarms and real-time manipulation of interactive objects, called 'phage'. These, illustrated in *The Phage* (2023) and inspired by the membrane-penetrating abilities of bacteriophage viruses, are collaborative physical instruments that allow the manipulation of virtual objects. Something between a game controller and a planchette, the instrument used for interfacing with the dead in séances since the late 18th century, each phage incorporates a microcontroller, sensors (heart rate, accelerometer, gyroscope, etc) and operates as a networked device, allowing several phage to work together for

collaborative control of virtual artefacts. Each phage has its own characteristics and behaviours, illuminating, listening, whispering, juddering or triggering events. They function as instruments to breach the membrane of the fulldome, allowing access to dimensions beyond.

Like the planchette, the phage allows communication with entities from the beyond. To date these have included: audience control of flocking boids (interactive animations driven by simple artificial intelligent behaviours); the incorporation of biometric sensors to access users' bodily states whilst interacting with virtual objects; and the use of sentiment analysis, such as IBM's Watson,[13] to incorporate emotional qualities interpreted from social media, text and conversational responses. The images *Phage Breaching the Fulldome Membrane* (2023) and *Phage Conjuring Ectoplasm* (2023) show the use of generative AI[14] to enable (almost) real-time image synthesis to generate digital ectoplasm through the manipulation of image parameters, such as hue, saturation, brightness and inversion, in order to increase interference in the rendering of new images. These algorithmic images were trained on an archive of images of ectoplasm and things morphologically similar to ectoplasm, before being sucked into a game-engine-driven fulldome environment. Phage can directly manipulate the emergence of Schwaiger's experimental ambitions, shifting any inadequate cinematic comparisons to real-time immersive performative experiences.

The fulldome is smothered in a digital ectoplasm. As well as the observable universe, the fulldome can manipulate physical, metaphysical and pataphysical matter through tangible digital interactions. The mythological, the divine and theological, the astronomical and astrological sit comfortably beside the Hertzian and the algorithmic in a spherical perspective. What better place to contemplate the immersive shock and awe of our own deaths. After all, ectoplasm is a matter somewhere between life and death. ⌂

Notes
1. Michael Powell and Emeric Pressburger (directors), *A Matter of Life and Death*, Eagle-Lion Films, 1946.
2. Gerry and Silvia Anderson (creators), *Fireball XL5* series, ITV, 1962.
3. JJ Abrams (director), *Star Trek*, Paramount Pictures, 2009.
4. Charles and Ray Eames (directors), *Powers of Ten*, IBM, 1977: https://www.eamesoffice.com/the-work/powers-of-ten/.
5. Camille Flammarion, *L'atmosphère: météorologie populaire*, Librairie Hachette (Paris), 1888, p 163.
6. See https://screenberry.com/.
7. Robert L Morris in a letter to the author, 21 October 1986.
8. Richard Fleischer (director), *Soylent Green*, Metro-Goldwyn-Mayer, 1973.
9. On the Immersive Vision Theatre, see https://i-dat.org/ivt/.
10. Bertie Charles Forbes, 'Edison Working on How to Communicate with the Next World', *American Magazine*, October 1920, p 10.
11. See https://i-dat.org/spectre-exhibition-by-mike-phillips/.
12. See https://i-dat.org/murmuration/.
13. See https://developer.ibm.com/components/watson-apis/.
14. On generative artificial intelligence, see Jeff Donahue and Karen Simonyan, 'Large-scale Adversarial Representation Learning', *Advances in Neural Information Processing Systems* 32, 2019, p 32.

Text © 2024 John Wiley & Sons Ltd. Images: pp 110–111, 116–17 © Mike Phillips, 2023. AI images generated using runwayml.com experimental BigBiGAN model; p 112 © ITV/Shutterstock; pp 114(b), 115 © Mike Phillips

Mark Morris

Piranesi
An Unsettling World of Architecture

The vastly overscaled elements, lineaments and sculptures of a seemingly infinite house form the backdrop of Susanna Clarke's 2020 novel *Piranesi*. Head of Teaching and Learning at the Architectural Association, **Mark Morris** draws on his research into architectural models, paracosms and the representation of buildings in fiction, filtering this through the lens of an encyclopaedic knowledge of architectural history to investigate the book's narrative arc, its ghostly visitations and its beautiful if not overbearing architectural *mise en scène*.

Giovanni Battista Piranesi,
The Smoking Fire,
Plate VI from *Carceri d'invenzione*,
1750
The first edition of 14 plates of Piranesi's *Carceri d'invenzione* (*Imaginary Prisons*) is looser and perhaps more atmospheric than the worked-over versions in the 1761 second edition. *The Smoking Fire* includes the tiered staircases and sense of architectural endlessness celebrated in Clarke's prose.

Giovanni Battista Piranesi, *The Pantheon, Interior,* from *Vedute di Roma,* 1768

As an archaeologist-artist, Piranesi documented the monuments of Rome in his series of etching portfolios *Vedute di Roma* (*Views of Rome*), the Pantheon a particular highlight. The view from the vestibule, just coming in from the portico, is particularly apt as Clarke names only Halls, Vestibules and Courtyards as composing Piranesi's world. The vestibule prepares for the scale of what it is to come, a space to prepare for more space.

The novelist Evelyn Waugh's author's note for his manor-house saga *Brideshead Revisited* (1945) is a knowing insurance policy intended to avoid autobiographical assumptions: 'I am not I: thou art not he or she: they are not they.'[1] It sets out the artifice of what is to come; class and religious worlds colliding. Yet the note suggests that autobiographical ambiguities are indeed present. Susanna Clarke's *Piranesi* (2020) plays with such ambiguities.[2] One could add a coda to Waugh's note, 'place is not place'. What is this haunting and memorable place that Clarke conjures? More gripping than the characters, of which there are only a handful, or the plot, which is artfully designed, it is the question of place that makes this stand out as a remarkable (architectural) novel.

Clarke deploys her own epigraph from *The Magician's Nephew* (1955) by CS Lewis: 'I am the great scholar, the magician, the adept, who is *doing* the experiment. Of course, I need subjects to do it on.'[3] One finds, two-thirds of the way into Clarke's book, that it is both the title character and the reader that are the subjects, the guinea pigs, who simultaneously come to realisations about the unique place described by the narrative. Whereas most works of fiction have a setting – a place in the world real or imagined – the architectural setting in *Piranesi* is the whole world. This alone captivates. The world of *Piranesi* is a seemingly infinite number of interior spaces: vast halls, vestibules, staircases. To occupy this world, referred to as the House, is to step into an etching by the artist, engraver and archaeologist who inspired the novel: Giovanni Battista Piranesi (1720–1778).

The first lines of the book set the tone and focus: 'When the moon rose in the Third Northern Hall I went to the Ninth Vestibule to witness the joining of three Tides. This is something that happens only once every eight years. The Ninth Vestibule is remarkable for the three great Staircases it contains. Its Walls are lined with marble Statues, hundreds upon hundreds of them, Tier upon Tier, rising into the distant heights.'[4]

The interiority of the fictional Piranesi's world is confirmed by reference to a confined outside, also architectural: 'The Windows of the House look out upon Great Courtyards, barren empty places paved with stone.'[5] Piranesi never ventures into the courtyards. The only things beyond these are the sun, moon and stars which allow for days and nights and keeping a calendar. Piranesi, largely alone, unquestioningly accepts this as his world, and seeks to better understand it: 'I am determined to explore as much of the World as I can in my lifetime. I have travelled as far as the Nine-Hundred-and-Sixtieth Hall to the West'.[6] There are three levels to Piranesi's world, connected by staircases: a lower level of tides, a middle level of men and birds, and an upper level of clouds. When anyone other than Piranesi appears in this world they are day-trippers from elsewhere, not of the House; ghosts of a kind.

In his depictions of the classical built environment, Giovanni Battista Piranesi created worlds so richly that those that took the Grand Tour at the instigation of his images were occasionally let down by the reality. The protagonist of Clarke's novel is called Piranesi derisively, as he is innocently unaware of the provenance of his surroundings. He attributes a benign quasi-religious sentience to the House: 'The Beauty of the House is immeasurable; its Kindness infinite.'[7] For Piranesi the House is Eden; 'May your Paths be safe, your Floors unbroken and may the House fill your eyes with Beauty.'[8] He fishes in its tides, contends with its birds, scrutinises the statues and keeps copious journal entries about it all, and these form the bulk of the narrative.

MC Escher,
Up and Down,
1947
Escher made a habit of taking study journeys or sketching holidays across Italy and Spain for inspiration, the tilework of the Alhambra in Granada being a major influence on his tessellation drawings. His last such journey included time at the mosque-cathedral at Córdoba, resulting in a number of architecturally focused works including *Up and Down*.

Unpacking, Unlocking

The House's spaces 'vary a great deal in the style of their Columns, Pilasters, Niches, Apses, Pediments etc., as well as in the number of their Doors and Windows',[9] which is to say they do not vary much at all in terms of a consistently applied classical grammar. Whilst Giovanni Battista Piranesi's well-known atmospheric etchings of imaginary prisons, the *Carceri d'invenzione* (c 1745–50), are a good place to start in picturing the environment of the novel in terms of their scale and unfathomable endlessness, the descriptions of the Halls and Vestibules more resemble other of his works, including drawings as well as etchings. Scale allows the architecture to stand in for landscape, much as those in the Middle Ages assumed ancient ruins were extensions of the landscape, sites to be scaled like cliffs or quarried for stone. Piranesi's *Vedute di Roma* (*Views of Rome*) also contribute, particularly interior views of the Pantheon (1768) and its portico (1757). The Pantheon, like the world of *Piranesi*, is a totalising space, a universe unto itself, with only the sun, moon and stars viewable through its dome's oculus.

As well as Piranesi's works, Clarke credits others as inspiration including MC Escher (1898–1972). His series of images inspired by the mosque-cathedral at Córdoba in Spain, like *Up and Down* (1947), combine staircases with columns, arcades and vaults in a manner more in sympathy with the novel. Beyond artwork, there are literary references, including knowing nods to CS Lewis's Narnia series (1950–56)[10] in respect to the statuary and the imaginary city of Charn, not to mention the slippage into other worlds and fading memories of the real world. Clarke also points to Jorge Luis Borges's short story 'The House of Asterion', first published in 1947, as a major influence. Borges ingeniously has the Minotaur narrate, describing in detail the wonders of his labyrinth and the reasons for his reclusion. 'All parts of the house are repeated many times, any place is another place. There is no one pool, courtyard, drinking trough, manger; the mangers, drinking troughs, courtyards pools are infinite in number. The house is the same size as the world; or rather it is the world.'[11] Just as with *Piranesi*, Borges allows the sun, moon and stars as being the only things beyond: 'Perhaps I have created the stars and the sun and this enormous house, but I no longer remember.'[12] The fading of the protagonist's memory is central to the plot of *Piranesi*.

Neil Spiller,
Summerson Series 1,
2022
right: One of a series in homage to John Summerson, architectural historian and director for 39 years of Sir John Soane's Museum, a place full of statues and architectural fragments. Statues in *Piranesi* infer the history of the House and allow the protagonist to project meaning and take shelter. 'Is it disrespectful to the House to love some Statues more than others? I sometimes ask Myself this question. It is my belief that the House itself loves and blesses equally everything that it has created' (*Piranesi*, p 17).

Neil Spiller,
Metaphysical Aedicule 3,
2021
opposite: Clarke's Piranesi takes refuge within enormous statues and hides in niches. *Metaphysical Aedicule 3* could describe so many of the nooks and crannies in vestibules and halls hinted at by Clarke. Spiller's layering of inky scrawls and fragmented figures collapses several aspects of *Piranesi* into one image, including journal pages, statuary, clouds and thresholds.

There is the question in both narratives regarding the realness of these built-up worlds. For Borges, the labyrinth is expanded beyond the notion of the maze into something like a vast palace – one that its host considers to be the world because he is trapped in it. Likewise, Clarke's Piranesi is found to be unknowingly trapped in the House, and ultimately escapes only to find that he misses his prison and the person he became there. Whereas the status of Borges's labyrinth is left ambiguously shrouded in myth, Clarke offers a dry-eyed distillation of the House's manifestation, describing it as a 'Distributary World' that is 'created by ideas flowing out of another world'.[13] Though this realisation is key to the plot's climax, the unpacking of the House as a manufactured realm or dreamscape spun from an undisclosed alternative world (likely our own) is befuddling. Many a reader by this point in the story will, like Piranesi, have fallen in love with his world, its architecture. Clarke rescues things by allowing Piranesi to return at will to the House as it constitutes part of his identity. There is a larger 'meta' point hinted at that all novels create worlds and that to escape to them is often a reader's fondest wish. Such authored worlds, realistic or fantastic, are accepted as part of one's willing suspension of disbelief to fully engage with the story.

Self-containment

But what exactly is this engagement? Is the House a solipsistic world created by the protagonist? No. Is solipsism – the idea that we all live in our own heads and build 'reality' individually – part of the novel's premise? Yes. Clarke wrote *Piranesi* during the Covid pandemic, homebound and suffering from chronic fatigue syndrome. She had seen much success with her debut novel, *Jonathan Strange and Mr Norrell* (2004).[14] Whereas that project was enthusiastically maximalist in terms of literary conceit and writing style, her follow-up was intensely focused, its prose, if not its premise, minimalist. Though the ideas underpinning *Piranesi* had been in hand long before Covid, it was the lockdown (an odd twinning of the world's predicament with her own foregoing seclusion) that propelled Clarke's writing, furtive and agonising though the process was. *Piranesi* can be viewed as a novel about being shut-in. Clarke's family describe her as self-contained. The House is any recluse's world; a management of agoraphobia by means of architecture, the interior standing in for exterior as a coping device; scale shifting to allow architecture to stand in for the world. Yet no matter how vast the architecture becomes, it remains claustrophobic – straining to breathe, searching for the sun, moon and stars to assert some wider measure of existence. *Piranesi* was a slow-burn project crafted in extremis. It had the nigh impossible task of following on from and being compared to Clarke's previous novel, not to mention the anticipation of 16 years between them. Despite this, it was a critical success, taking the 2021 Women's Prize for Fiction.

James Casebere,
Nevisian Underground 1,
2001
right: Casebere's painstaking photography work with scale models included in 2001 a series of flooded interiors, a theme to which he has recently returned. Such images could well represent the lower levels in *Piranesi* or indeed when the Tides rise to the middle level – always noted as a special event in the fictional Piranesi's journals.

James Casebere,
Yellow Hallway 2,
2001
below: Casebere achieves his watery effects with clear resin. His 'Yellow Hallway' series could easily illustrate a dramatic scene in Clarke's novel: 'Vast quantities of Water poured into surrounding Halls, including the one where the Other was. The Waters plucked him up and carried him away, sweeping him through Doors and battering him against Walls and Statues' (*Piranesi*, p 25).

Within a contemporary discourse around worldbuilding, literary forerunners are nearly all about imaginary islands, continents, planets. The *worldness* of worlds persists in worldbuilding reaching back to Jonathan Swift's *Gulliver's Travels* of 1726. In subverting expectations throughout her novel, Clarke inverts worldbuilding to building-as-world; JRR Tolkien's maps of Middle-earth are replaced by an architectural plan. Clarke credits Tolkien's *The Lord of the Rings* (1954–5)[15] with helping her draft *Jonathan Strange and Mr Norrell*. To flip that fantasy world inside out as a basis for her next novel reveals a cool logic. In so doing, she arrived at a genuinely unique contribution to architecture and literature. Asterion's world seems total, but is not really; Piranesi's is, for good or ill. And illness must be credited with contributing to the creation of Piranesi's building world. If the genres of imaginary worlds are considered, *Piranesi* is less solipsistic and more akin to a paracosm: a parallel world crafted in the imagination over a long span of time, a world with its own carefully worked-out characteristics. The future novelist sisters Charlotte, Emily and Anne Brontë famously shared paracosms as generators of their early stories during their Yorkshire childhood in the 1820s. Clarke's paracosmic setting occasionally seems itself a character, and is for much of the book inseparable from the narrative.

James Casebere,
Piranesi Prison,
1995
Casebere started a model inspired by Piranesi's *Carceri d'invenzione*. A Polaroid study looked at composition, cropping and lighting. Though never finalised as a project, the model – stripped of architectural details – powerfully conveys the bigger spatial moves implied by Piranesi's etchings – 3D from 2D.

Piranesi's awkward relationship with another character, called 'the Other', who regularly visits but does not live in Piranesi's world, finally prompts him to question the basis of their interactions focused on rituals intended to extricate some profound learning: 'I realised that the search for the Knowledge has encouraged us to think of the House as if it were a sort of riddle to be unravelled, a text to be interpreted, and that if ever we discover the Knowledge, then it will be as if the Value has been wrested from the House and all that remains will be mere scenery.' This prompts a revelation, a defence of architecture: 'The sight of the One-Hundred-and-Ninety-Second Western Hall in the Moonlight made me see how ridiculous that is. The House is valuable because it is the House. It is enough in and of Itself. It is not the means to an end.'[16]

Mere scenery or setting it cannot be, because scenery and setting are nearly everything in *Piranesi*. The protagonist's ability to access this other world is also Clarke's, so complete is this paracosm derived from scant ingredients. The abiding gift of the novel is that any reader may do so as well. In this sense, for many, *Piranesi* produces an after-effect; its spaces so copiously explored, it flutters through one's imagination long after being read. The House sticks in the mind, and opens itself up to visits from many other Others. ⌂

Notes
1. Evelyn Waugh, *Brideshead Revisited: The Sacred and Profane Memories of Captain Charles Ryder*, Chapman & Hall (London), 1945, p 4.
2. Susanna Clarke, *Piranesi*, Bloomsbury (London), 2020.
3. CS Lewis, *The Magician's Nephew*, The Bodley Head (London), 1955, p 26.
4. Clarke, *Piranesi*, op cit, p 3.
5. *Ibid*, p 6.
6. *Ibid*, p 5.
7. *Ibid*.
8. *Ibid*, p 92.
9. *Ibid*, p 47.
10. CS Lewis, *The Chronicles of Narnia*, 7 vols originally published individually between 1950 and 1956 by Geoffrey Bles and then The Bodley Head, and since 1994 by HarperCollins (New York).
11. Jorge Luis Borges, 'The House of Asterion', in Donald Yates and James Irby (eds), *Labyrinths: Selected Stories and Other Writings*, Penguin (London), p 171.
12. *Ibid*, p 172.
13. Clarke, *Piranesi*, op cit, p 89.
14. Susanna Clarke, *Jonathan Strange and Mr Norrell*, Bloomsbury (London), 2004.
15. JRR Tolkien, *The Lord of the Rings*, 3 vols originally published 1954–5 by Allen & Unwin (London).
16. Clarke, *Piranesi*, op cit, p 60.

Text © 2024 John Wiley & Sons Ltd. Images: p 121 MC Escher's 'Up and Down' © 2024 The M.C. Escher Company – The Netherlands. All rights reserved. www.mcescher.com; pp 122–23 © Neil Spiller; pp 124–5 Courtesy James Casebere and Sean Kelly Gallery

Michael Chapman

HARD SPIRI

ARCHITECTURAL APPARITIONS IN HAYAO MIYAZAKI'S *SPIRITED AWAY*

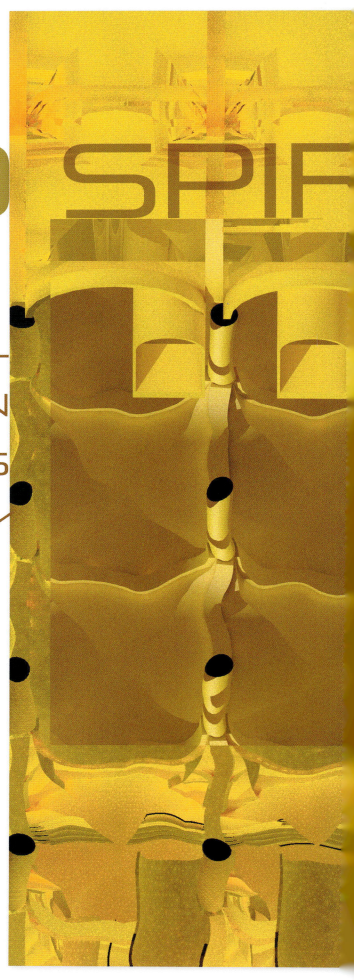

Michael Chapman,
Entry Hall, 'Spirit' series,
2023

left: Drawn from the spatial imagery of Surrealism, and the hallucinogenic images of Salvador Dalí in particular, the axonometric mapping of the entry hall interior creates a series of illusions in scale and depth using reflection to show multiple aspects of the architectural space and narrative simultaneously.

opposite: The plan drawing re-creates the internal geometry and terrain of the entry hall in Hayao Miyazaki's *Spirited Away* (2001) in a reconstructed aerial perspective that positions the architecture and its contextual landscape as it features in the narrative.

FILM HAS A LONG HISTORY OF SPECTRAL ASSOCIATION, FROM THE POSSIBILITIES OF PROJECTION, THE DANCING IMAGE THAT HANGS IN THE AIR, TO THE TRANSLUCENCE OF THE MEDIA ITSELF. TAKING INSPIRATION FROM A JAPANESE ANIMATION, MICHAEL CHAPMAN, PROFESSOR AND CHAIR OF ARCHITECTURE AND INDUSTRIAL DESIGN AT WESTERN SYDNEY UNIVERSITY, HAS CREATED A SERIES OF WORKS THAT SEEK TO FILL IN THE HAUNTED BLANKS AND UNCANNY PARALLAXES THAT EXIST BETWEEN THE SPACE WE VIEW AND PERCEIVE IN THE FILMIC SEQUENCE AND AN 'OBJECTIVE' REALITY OF THAT ARCHITECTURE. HE USES SOME OF THE COMPOSITIONAL PROTOCOLS OF THE TRADITIONAL SCROLL AND MACHINERY TO PRODUCE HIS PROPOSAL — A PARALLEL WORLD THAT HAUNTS THE ABSENCES AND HOLES WITHIN THE ORIGINAL.

Hayao Miyazaki,
Film still of the bath house interior in *Spirited Away*, 2001
Peopled by all manner of folkloric figures, lost spirits and uncanny characters, the bath house is one of the primary locations for the supernatural events in the film. Its form can be seen to draw inspiration from the traditional Sentō typology long connected with Buddhism's ritual cleansing.

Released in 2001, Hayao Miyazaki's *Spirited Away* is a Studio Ghibli animated film which interweaves traditional architectural typologies with Japanese folklore in a way that specifically engages with supernatural phenomena as a spatial condition. Two key typologies – the entry hall and the bath house – provide the backdrop to the central character Chihiro Ogino's journey from the everyday world into one inhabited and endlessly reshaped by ghostly spirits. There is a rich history of ghosts in Japanese culture, as well as the vast pantheon of spirits that permeate the Shinto-Buddhist cosmology and are frequently depicted in the narrative form of the scroll, which positions figures in both time and space through drawing.

As well as these metaphysical and representational devices, the film also contains an allegorical critique of contemporary Japanese society where machine and industrialised forms start to influence the traditional spatial forms in both the plot and its architecture.

What is unique about Miyazaki's animation of *Spirited Away* is that the architecture is given spatial, temporal and anthropomorphic qualities that reveal an original, and largely unexplored architecture which is inherently incomplete, while

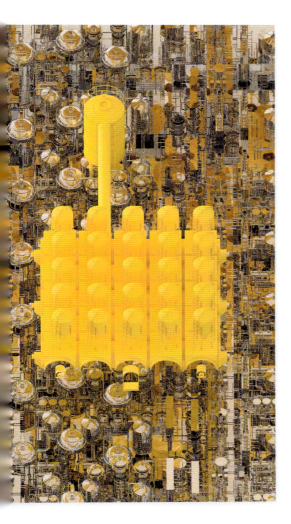

Michael Chapman,
Entry Hall, 'Spirit' series,
2023
Axonometric projection is used to create the narrative sequence through the entry hall as a machinery of industrial parts, extracting elements of the Japanese scroll to position time and memory in relation to the filmic sequence.

overladen with residual legacies. Using the conventions of architectural drawing, and specifically the frontal axonometric model of the Japanese scroll, the 'Spirit' series of drawings here documents the architecture of the entry hall and bath house in all its supernatural forms using found elements from industrial and machine forms. Truncating these fictional architectures from their filmic context, this process explores the voids and contradictions concealed within the narrative form of film, but made evident through forensic architectural documentation. Frozen in time, the drawings attempt to shift the emphasis away from the dominant plot narrative, towards hidden and disguised narratives that are concealed in the film, but open onto larger supernatural themes within Japanese culture and its architecture.

Animation is a visual process that, by assembling constantly changing images in a state of rapid motion, creates an immersive or living world that can be visually inhabited, and layered with emotion. The drawings set out to use mapping techniques to ossify the built elements and their landscape in order to extract an architecture from the filmic narratives that are woven through it. They reverse-engineer animation to extract an architecture. The intention was to draw on the traditions of Japanese scrolls, but with unemotional industrial forms that deliberately fill the voids or blindspots not revealed in the sequence. This mapping is able to assimilate the collisions in scale, time, space and gravity that underpin the original architectures, creating a ghosted trace of the film and its emotional residue. Focusing on moments of entry, scale and structure, the 'Spirit' drawings make a clear distinction between the architectural and natural world, deploying a language of using found industrialised forms to fill in the cinematic blanks. Reassembling two of the key structures in the opening stages of *Spirited Away*, this approach creates a geometry and notational sequence in both time and space that is then reimagined as fictional filmic monuments. If the animated sequence uses a fictional architecture as a backdrop to film, this mapping sets out to create an architectural structure for a fictional and non-existent film. This uninhabited world is haunted by the ghosts of *Spirited Away* and its silent narratives, which are both recalled and remembered.

The Entry Hall
The narrative sequence of *Spirited Away* starts with a family moving cities to create a new life. On the way they discover a ruined and abandoned theme park where they stop to explore. Despite the child's reservations, the parents enter a long tunnel and discover a dark, vaulted space in the bowels of a large building. In the 'Spirit' drawing series, this is the *Entry Hall*, as it is the entrance to both the park and the film's storyline. From the outside, looking back, the structure is a vast monolithic building sitting on a steep landscape. From inside, it is intimate and has a Piranesian labyrinthine quality, reinforced by its repetition and symmetry. While the narrative moves through these vaulted catacombs, there are bodily and visual entry points (or exits) to the world the family is leaving, and also arriving into. In this sense, the space has a metaphysical quality acting as a witness to events and a container for ritual and memory.

THE TRADITIONAL ARCHITECTURE OF THE BATH HOUSE CREATES A SERIES OF LAYERED TIERS THAT GROW OUT OF THE ROCKY LANDSCAPE GIVING IT THE SENSE OF AN ISLAND

The drawings try to position the known elements of the entry hall within a fictional and changing animated world. Using the tunnel, windows and exit door as a starting point, the mapping re-creates the vaults and their incompatibilities. The unvisited parts of the architecture are represented through found industrial objects that replicate the scale but not the form of the represented structure. As the family exits the structure and wanders up the hill, the building looks back at them with hauntingly anthropomorphic qualities. The mappings position the structure within its landscape as an apparition of the fictional sequence, but also anchored in its own reality. The drawings borrow from the structure of Japanese scrolls to imagine the same sequence from multiple points of view – and simultaneously – in order to demonstrate, and also blur, what is known and unknown.

The Bath House
The entry hall and the bath house are divided by a street, furnished with a mysterious left-behind banquet. As Chihiro's parents consume the food, she is overcome with anxiety, leaving to explore. At the end of the street a bridge appears, and beyond the bridge is the bath house, labelled in the English subtitles. The ominous structure glares back at Chihiro, from where she can visually reconstruct its relationship to the landscape as an infrastructure of oil production. The traditional architecture of the bath house creates a series of layered tiers

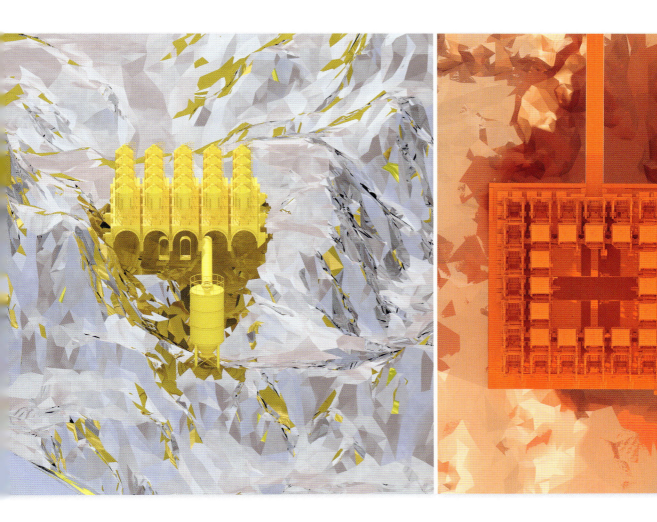

that grow out of the rocky landscape giving it the sense of an island. The mood of the bath house is more foreboding in this sequence, and the scale even more confronting. In the opening sequences, little of the interior is revealed, but the physiognomy of the façade is clearly menacing. As the child approaches the structure, the mood dramatically changes, surging forward with spirits and ghosts that force her to flee. As she returns to her parents, who have now consumed the banquet, she finds they have been transformed into pigs, and that the food was sacred, for an offering which they transgressed. The remainder of the film unravels this conundrum, frequently shifting between adult and child, and animal and human.

Michael Chapman,
Entry Hall, 'Spirit'
series,
2023

opposite: Sectional-elevational mapping of the passage from the car (represented as the silo) to the exit of the entry hall, positioned in the landscape and in relation to the primary windows and exits.

above left: Re-creating the entry hall in elevation as a continuation of its landscape, the drawing represents the full transition of the characters through the interior spaces represented in the film, from entry to exit. The elevation re-creates the expanded exterior landscape the architecture sits within.

Michael Chapman,
Bath House, 'Spirit'
series,
2023
above right: The plan drawing of the bath house positions the architecture within a reconstructed landscape, from the bridge to the interior courtyard.

Michael Chapman,
Bath House, 'Spirit' series,
2023

right: Inspired by the romantic sublime, the frontal elevation uses the techniques of the Japanese scroll to spatially construct the process of leaving the natural landscape to enter the monolithic island of the bath house.

opposite top: The sectional-elevation reconstructs the transition depicted in the film, from the natural landscape to the machinic and ghostly world of the bath house, positioning the architecture within its expanded context.

Arata Isozaki,
Tsukaba Center Building #2,
Tsukaba, Japan,
1985

opposite bottom: Purportedly unsatisfied with the lacking cultural and narrative capacities of contemporary architecture, Japanese architect Arata Isozaki famously created a set of drawings depicting his then new Tsukaba Center Building (1983) in ruins, offering the building a life beyond the immediacy of its completion.

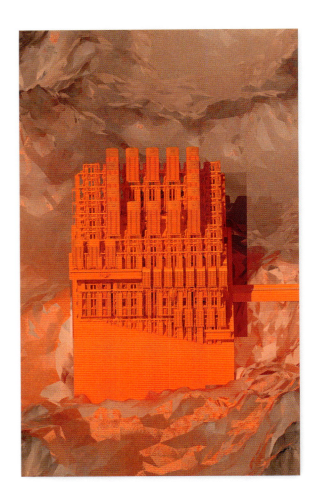

The mapping of the bath house sets to capture the implied dialogue between the interior and exterior, again using repeated industrial forms to assemble the elements. The mass of the building, and its relationship to a landscape that is being transformed beneath it, is central to the plot and reconstructed in the architecture. The *Bath House* drawings use elevational and axonometric treatments, again in reference to spatial structures of the scroll to position the architectural narrative within its fictional terrain. The entry sequence, bridge and fenestration provide the key to the known elements of the exterior, but also frame the events of the interior where a vast array of spirits and ghosts have been entombed. The architecture provides a constantly shifting backdrop to the narrative, and also a filmic device through which it is recorded. As with the entry hall, the bath house functions as a witness to events and rituals. As the architecture is removed from this context, it offers a ghosting of these memories from multiple lenses. Inspired by the mood of the original structure, the drawings aim to capture an emotional state and foreboding, even without the characters that construct it.

Ruins of a Film

While the narrative of *Spirited Away* is framed by these two architectural extremes, it also creates a window into a broader critique of Japanese and capitalist culture in the 1980s, and director Miyazaki's own Marxist tendencies. He described this in 2005 through the binary between nature and the physical world, arguing that 'money and desire – all that is going to collapse, and wild green grasses are going to take over'.[1] The film tells this story of ruination, and positions architecture in a sequence of time and degradation where even the known cannot be trusted. These same themes come together in Arata Isozaki's scroll-like drawings of the Tsukaba Center Building (1983), depicted as a deconstructed ruin. Strongly referencing traditional techniques, Isozaki uses the medium of drawing to offer alternate perspectives of the same reality, which unsettles and disrupts the known facts. This process has a resonance with the dreamlike animations of Miyazaki, which also lead us through the real and the fictional to create new forms of ghosted memories.

The process of retracing the narratives of the entry hall and bath house in the 'Spirit' drawings, through a forensic reconstruction of the architecture in *Spirited Away*, leaves behind a memory or trace of the mythical world that anchors the film, but is also floating mysteriously away in both time and space. The drawings use architecture to engage the memory of a film, where residues of the narrative occupy the work in the same ethereal way. These warring

THE ARCHITECTURE PROVIDES A CONSTANTLY SHIFTING BACKDROP TO THE NARRATIVE, AND ALSO A FILMIC DEVICE THROUGH WHICH IT IS RECORDED

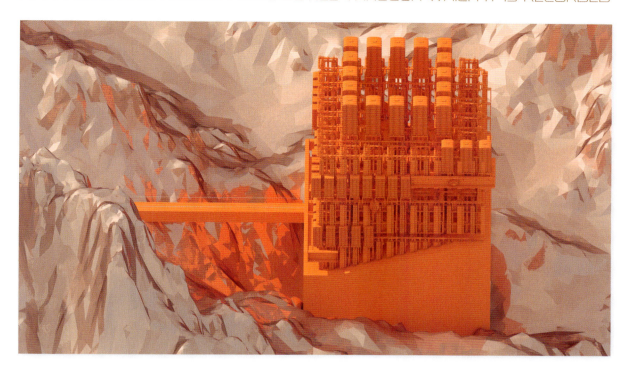

fictions look to translate the world of architecture and film to create a mutual understanding or discourse where each haunts the other. The interplay between time and space – constantly moving in the film and frozen in the architecture – is a known representational device of the traditional scroll, which provides the script for these twisted apparitions and the key to unlocking them. Similarly, the landscapes that are trespassed in the film are entombed within the architecture, creating inviting entry into this metaphysical architectonic terrain, sandwiched between the entry and exits of these mysterious worlds without horizon. 𝄞

Note
1. Hayao Miyazaki, quoted in Margaret Talbot, 'The Auteur of Anime: A Visit with the Elusive Genius Hayao Miyazaki', *The New Yorker*, 9 January 2005, p 75.

Text © 2024 John Wiley & Sons Ltd. Images: pp 126–7, 129–32, 133(t) © Michael Chapman; p 128 © Studio Ghibli/Kobal/Shutterstock; p 133(b) © Estate of Arata Isozaki

FROM ANOTHER PERSPECTIVE *A Word from D Editor Neil Spiller*

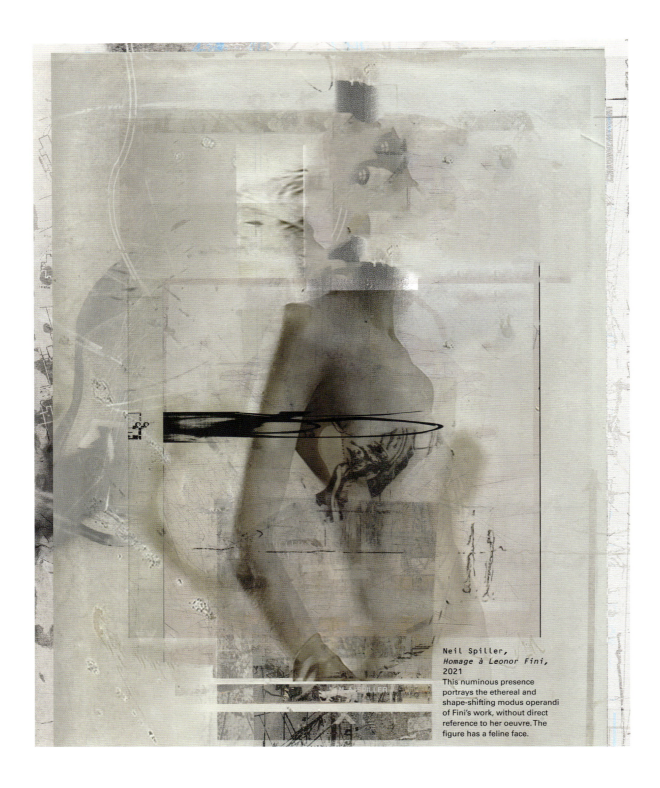

Neil Spiller, *Homage à Leonor Fini*, 2021
This numinous presence portrays the ethereal and shape-shifting modus operandi of Fini's work, without direct reference to her oeuvre. The figure has a feline face.

BEYOND THE REALMS OF DEATH

A manipulative Harlequin slipping through the alleys and twitterns between one world and another, one supernatural realm and another, one age and another weaving what at close perspective sometimes seems a chaotic course.
— Michael Moorcock, 1995[1]

Creativity is like a Harlequin, at once demonic yet also cheeky. For the creative, the big fear is that one might never see the Harlequin again or tread its meandering, time-travelling paths or séance with its attendant ghosts. So when it comes, you must let it lead you wherever it wishes to take you. This piece is about some of places the Harlequin has led me recently and the ghosts I have communed with – a world of strange chimeric bodies, harsh geometries of love, a eulogy and six pages in search of a book and author.

A Play Within a Play
In 1921, Luigi Pirandello premiered his highly experimental play *Six Characters in Search of an Author*. Six characters from his previously aborted, draft plays invade a rehearsal for another play, searching for a director to stage their life stories. The relationship between the rehearsing actors and the invasive characters deteriorates and becomes antagonistic as they discuss and argue notions so crucial to theatre and indeed existence itself: What is art? What is reality? What is creativity?

After the Second World War it was difficult for people to connect as fully as before with concepts of morality and meaning. Continuing urbanisation and industrialisation made it hard for individuals to define their personal identity. This was also true in terms of architectural practice which was engulfed by the dogmas, doctrines and diktats of architectural Modernism. To break the mould was seen as tantamount to applying to be a resident of the madhouse – outside time and space, forever a ghost. In my work, particularly in the last 40 years, the Harlequin has become much more welcome, intrepid and emboldened.

In my first attempt to make a book layout and design (BLAD) as a taster for a possible publication for my long-standing and continuing 'Communicating Vessels' project (1998–), the graphic designers v23 (Vaughan Oliver and Chris Bigg) and I alighted on the idea similar to Pirandello's play of creating a book within a book – a user's manual more opaque than the already surreal project around it.

Even before the making of the BLAD, the Harlequin pointed to the ghost of Gian Lorenzo Bernini and cultivated an appreciation of his 17th-century works, both sculpture and architecture, in Rome. Whilst in the city's Piazza Barberini (named after Pope Urban VIII whose family name was Barberini), I came across a Bernini-designed, modest, clamshell-shaped horse-trough fountain. The Fontana delle Api features a bee at its centre, out of which a single spurt of replenishing water continuously pours. The Barberini family crest previously sported horseflies but these were considered too unwelcoming and were later replaced by bees. The bee is a symbol of regal aspirations.

On another time-travelling trajectory, my chequered-costumed guide pushed me towards an interest in the French enigmatic artist and lover of the chequered chessboard, Marcel Duchamp.

In 1913, Duchamp was starting to conceive his great work *The Bride Stripped Bare by Her Bachelors, Even* (1915–23) – often known as *The Large Glass*. In August that year, he arrived in Herne Bay, Kent, to chaperone his sister who was learning English there. Herne Bay is a quiet seaside town a couple of miles from the small village of Fordwich, the 'site' – another coincidental resonance orchestrated by the Harlequin – of my 'Communicating Vessels' island. Whilst in Herne Bay, Duchamp made four sketches, two of which were entitled *Wasp, or Sex Cylinder*. These were the basis of what was to become the 'Bride' in the top left-hand part of the *Glass*.

Contemporary artist Jeremy Millar made a speculative film in 2006 about what might have inspired Duchamp's use of *Wasp* and the sash-window form (rare on the continent but in abundance in Herne Bay) in *The Large*

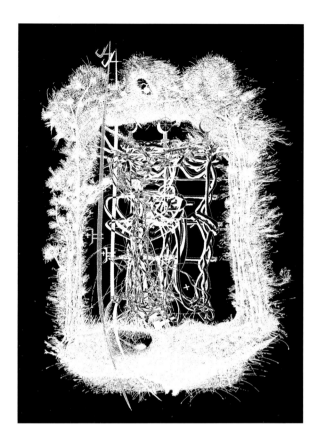

Neil Spiller,
Bee Gate seen through the Holey Hedge,
'Communicating Vessels' series,
2019
left: Bees and wasps naturally occur on the 'Communicating Vessels' island, attracted by its verdant plants. The project choreographs the movements and translates them into wispy gates that slowly disappear.

Glass. Millar writes: 'As my film is about the possible discovery made by a fictional character researching Duchamp in Herne Bay, I began to speculate what this might be. Perhaps the rare colony of digger wasps found a mile or so along the coast, and especially active during August, might provide a […] plausible explanation for the appearance of the word wasp in the title of two of Duchamp's drawings'.[2]

In reference and respect for these two ghostly great artists, separated by centuries in time, 'Communicating Vessels' features bees and wasps. They are everywhere on the tiny island in Fordwich: aero-gel wispy gates are created from their flight patterns (mapped by computers) that disperse like cigarette smoke in the breeze. Bees also appear in the pages of the BLAD.

Neil Spiller,
Choose your Weapons: Harsh Geometries of Love,
'Communicating Vessels' series,
2019
opposite: A double-page spread from the last version of the projected *Communicating Vessels* book – *The Harsh Geometries of Love* is the name of the book within the book. A variety of weapons are featured including Bernini's *Ecstasy of St Teresa* (1652).

Neil Spiller,
Numinous Presence 6,
2021
right: Much of the work utilises the book-inside-a-book idea; this drawing predicated the frame-within-a-frame notion, which allows the drawing to highlight its own important centre.

Neil Spiller,
Dalinian Leg and Archaeological Slam,
2019
opposite. This double-page spread was made as an example of the juxtaposition of drawings that add new relationships between and within the work, using the book as a kaleidoscopic device.

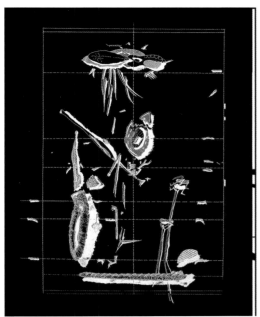
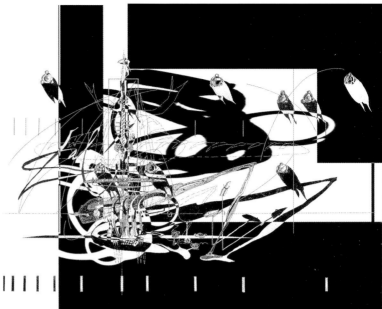

Chimeric Bodies and Cats' Eyes
Another creative dance with the Harlequin made me make a series of works that communed with a triumvirate of 20th-century ghosts: Argentinian-Italian artist Leonor Fini, Catalan artist Salvador Dalí and English jazz and blues singer, artist and critic George Melly.

The characters in Fini's art were always female and androgynous. Her figures are chimeric, often inspired by Greek goddesses. She sought depictions of femininity that could not be stereotyped by the male gaze, which was often her motivation to be the subject of her work in various feline masks and surreal gloves. Like many Surrealists, Dalí was obsessed with the eye, its blinding and the denial of the ocular-centric world in favour of the hybrid phantoms of the dream state. The third element in this particular graphic odyssey was a book of prose by Melly, with fantastic photographs by Michael Woods of the quirkier side of Paris – mannequin shops, ancient stocking emporiums, antiquated arcades and monuments – stressing the city's Surrealist heritage in moody black-and-white prints.[3]

My own resulting works have a spectral quality, brimming with an ambiguous ectoplasmic presence.

Pages in Search of a Book
Over the years there have been many attempts to publish a book of the 'Communicating Vessels'. The most recent, again working with the late Vaughan Oliver, entailed confronting my own drawing ghosts and wondering whether the Harlequin would return and could squeeze more juice out of the project. The answer was yes, but unfortunately Vaughan died before we could put all our plans into action and produce the book. What remains are ghosts of ideas, fortuitous juxtapositions and graphic swerves caught in limbo, some sort of designer's purgatory, neither cast to Hell nor elevated to Heaven – in the waiting room, expiating.

Neil Spiller,
Possible cover for
'*Communicating Vessels*' series,
2019
above and opposite: These double-page spreads were made to inspire Vaughan Oliver – he never saw them. I was looking forward to a resumption of our fun and creative collaboration, but it never came.

Dear Vaughan,

It's twenty-two years since we met in your studio in Battersea: a temple to creativity, the v23 velocipede of graphic love – big, big love. I was told: 'You need Vaughan' and you came out from behind your desk in a corner. We instantly recognised ourselves in each other: our professional deviance – iconoclastic and maverick – mine in architecture, yours as an artisan of sonic tapestry wrapping. Our deep love of Surrealism; our great love of books, especially ones we had made (we didn't make enough of those together). Our dry but forever lateral humour, our fathers involved with the Coal Board, our education at roughly the same time in the Poly's. Our fatherhood – we each had two boys. However you took it too far with Sunderland FC, though I forgive you!

We found out that we lived at the end of the same street in Wandsworth. You took that as a sign of benign creative fate – and you were right.

Over the years you have been nothing but a hero to me: baulking at imbecilic academics, keeping your integrity intact, and producing fantastic work after fantastic work – nothing ever was a minger! Popping into my office, usually unannounced, always a wonderful surprise, with a 'How are you bonny lad?' followed by a hug and a belly bump.

We've shared some fantastic meals, had more than a few drinks (those bellies needed maintaining) and the three of us – you, me and Lee [Vaughan's wife] – have had so many laughs. You've told the funniest jokes, all gleaned from life, which have had me spitting out my drink with the sheer surprise of it all way too often. We've talked for hours of many things: high brow and low brow, serious and frivolous, through days and nights.

I feel deeply honoured that I've known Vaughan Oliver the man, father, husband, lunch companion, creative collaborator and benign, beautiful mentalist and diamond geezer and called you one of my best friends and, shockingly, I felt it reciprocated. We were simply tuned into each other's emotional wavelength.

There is indeed more beauty in the world because of you and it has touched me along with many, many thousands, if not millions, of others. The outpouring of love for you on social media is astonishing and well deserved.

Vaughan Oliver, I love you and nothing is ever going to change that.

— Eulogy written by Neil Spiller for the funeral of Vaughan Oliver (1957–2019), London, 31 January 2020

Ink Soaked Boy

Communicating Vessels

Vaughan Oliver, renowned graphic designer, was indeed a Harlequin, popping up intermittently with a joke and a cheeky grin, demonic wit and a plethora of extraordinary ideas. I often commune with his ghost and we talk beyond the realms of death. I remind him he still has my favourite Bernini book! ⌂

Notes
1. Michael Moorcock describing Iain Sinclair in his 1995 Afterword to Iain Sinclair, *Lud Heat* [1975], Skylight Press (Cheltenham), 2012, p 137.
2. Jeremy Millar, 'Looking Through the Large Glass: Marcel Duchamp in England', *Tate Etc* 7, Summer 2006: www.tate.org.uk/tate-etc/issue-7-summer-2006/looking-through-large-glass.
3. George Melly, *Paris and the Surrealists*, Thames & Hudson (London), 1991.

Text © 2024 John Wiley & Sons Ltd.
Images © Neil Spiller

GHOST STORIES
ARCHITECTURE AND THE INTANGIBLE

Kirsty Badenoch is an artist, architect, researcher and educator with 10 years' experience with leading landscape architecture and urbanism practices across Europe. Her work interrogates situations of ecological justice through interdisciplinary and collaborative site-based projects, centring on fragile and disturbed landscapes. She teaches at the Bartlett School of Architecture, University College London (UCL), is Head of Research at Periscope, and curator of Microscope.

Michael Chapman is Professor and Chair of Architecture and Industrial Design at Western Sydney University. He has written widely about all aspects of architectural drawing and theory, with a particular focus on Dada and Surrealism. His creative work has been widely exhibited and published, and he is a co-author of *Residue: Architecture as a Condition of Loss* (RMIT Press, 2007).

Nat Chard is Professor of Experimental Architecture at the Bartlett School of Architecture, UCL, following professorships at the Royal Danish Academy in Copenhagen, University of Manitoba and the University of Brighton. He is an architect registered in the UK and has practised in London. His work has been published and exhibited internationally. His research practice develops means of discussing uncertain conditions in architecture, and recent work has been acted out through a series of drawing instruments.

Daniel Dream is an architectural designer, researcher and educator. He has taught and practised in Beijing, Hong Kong and London. His work has been published and exhibited internationally, and he currently teaches undergraduate and postgraduate design studios at the Bartlett School of Architecture, UCL, and at the University of Greenwich. Central to his research are explorations of different conceptions of the architectural practitioner in relation to interplays of sculpture, publishing and fiction.

Oliver G Goché is an artist and designer. His sensibilities for the work come from living in the Iowan landscape, specifically focusing on spatially driven potentials in the manner of drawing and assembly, and the study of phenomena, and how these drive the world around us.

Peter P Goché is a practising architect, artist and educator, and founder of Black Contemporary, a rural field station dedicated to the study of atmospheric logic and perception. Using site-adjusted installations as a primary mode of practice, he deploys an integrated approach to both theoretical and practical questions pertaining to the nature and impact of materiality specific to the reoccupation of post-industrial spaces. His research on material practices has been published in a number of edited books and journals, including *Architecture as a Performing Art* (Ashgate, 2013) and *Architecture and Culture* (vol 4, no 3, 2016). He also co-led workshops at the 2014 and 2018 Venice Architecture Biennale.

Perry Kulper is an architect and professor of architecture at Taubman College, University of Michigan. He holds various international visiting teaching positions and professorships, including the prestigious Sir Bannister Fletcher Visiting Professorship at the Bartlett School of Architecture, UCL (2019). His diverse interests include architectural pedagogy, design methods and architecture's expanding constituencies of care, which he frames, through both his practice and teaching, as architecture's cultural imagination. In 2013 he co-authored (with Nat Chard) *Pamphlet Architecture 34: Fathoming the Unfathomable, Archival Ghosts and Paradoxical Shadows*.

Ifigeneia Liangi is an architectural designer, researcher and educator. She is a lecturer at the Bartlett School of Architecture, UCL, and at the University of Greenwich, London. Her work has been exhibited in various places including the Royal Academy of Arts in London and the Michael Cacoyiannis Foundation in Athens. Central to her research are considerations on the links between architecture and storytelling. She has practised in both the UK and Greece.

Eva Menuhin is a writer, editor, copy-editor and translator with expertise in art, academic and architectural subjects. Her experience includes collaborating with the late Sir Philip Dowson, Ian Ritchie, the Architectural Association (AA) School of

CONTRIBUTORS

Architecture, Stufish Entertainment Architects and writing for 𝘋. She studied Italian and Linguistics at Stanford University, California, and has been based in London for the past 25 years.

Mark Morris is Head of Teaching and Learning at the Architectural Association (AA) where he lectures in History and Theory Studies. His research focuses on questions of visual representation, particularly the role of scale models, in the context of the history of architectural education. For the last decade he has also looked at architectural novels, organising seminars on the topic at Cornell University in Ithaca, New York, and at the AA. He is the author of two books: *Models: Architecture and the Miniature* (Academy Press, 2006) and *Automatic Architecture: Designs from the Fourth Dimension* (College of Architecture, 2004), and is guest-editor (with Mike Aling) of 𝘋 *Worldmodelling: Architectural Models in the 21st Century* (May/June 2021).

Mike Phillips is Professor of Interdisciplinary Arts at the University of Plymouth, and the Director of Research at i-DAT.org. His research and development orbits a portfolio of projects that explore the ubiquity of data 'harvested' from an instrumentalised world and its potential as a material for revealing things that lie outside our normal frames of reference – things so far away, so close, so massive, so small and so ad infinitum. He manages the Fulldome Immersive Vision Theatre, a transdisciplinary instrument for manifesting (im)material and imaginary worlds, and is a founding Partner of FullDome UK.

Ian Ritchie is the director of ritchie*studio, a practice that has won over a hundred national and international awards. He is a Royal Academician, member of the Akademie der Künste Berlin, and Member of the Politecnico di Milano Academic Board. He has chaired many international juries, including for the Stirling Prize and Berlin Art Prize, and has received major international innovation awards. He lectures internationally at conferences and universities, and his art on paper is in the collections of several major galleries and museums. He has 'landed' two recent sculptures at Arte Sella: the contemporary mountain. He writes poetry and books. Recent books include *Renewal Architects* and *Light*, both published by Unicorn in 2023.

Chris Speed is Professor of Design for Regenerative Futures at RMIT University, Melbourne, where he collaborates with a wide variety of partners to explore how design provides methods to adapt and create products and services towards a regenerative society. He has an established track record in directing large complex grants with academic, industry and third-sector partners that apply design and data methods to social, environmental and economic challenges.

Neil Spiller is Editor of 𝘋, and was previously Hawksmoor Chair of Architecture and Landscape and Deputy Pro Vice Chancellor at the University of Greenwich in London. Prior to this he was Vice Dean at the Bartlett School of Architecture, UCL. He has made an international reputation as an architect, designer, artist, teacher, writer and polemicist. He is the founding director of the Advanced Virtual and Technological Architecture Research (AVATAR) group, which continues to push the boundaries of architectural design and discourse in the face of the impact of 21st-century technologies. Its current preoccupations include augmented and mixed realities and other metamorphic technologies.

Cameron Stebbing is an architectural designer whose work explores the speculative potential of architectural conservation practices and the capacity of its documentary methods to explore uncertain chronological frames and ethical positions. He graduated with his Part I from the University of Lincoln in 2019 and his Part II from the University of Huddersfield in 2023. His work won the RIBA East Midlands Student of the Year prize in 2019, and he has had projects nominated for the RIBA Bronze, Silver and Dissertation medals. He currently works at Donald Insall Associates in York.

What is *Architectural Design*?

Founded in 1930, *Architectural Design* (△) is an influential and prestigious publication. It combines the currency and topicality of a newsstand journal with the rigour and production qualities of a book. With an almost unrivalled reputation worldwide, it is consistently at the forefront of cultural thought and design.

Issues of △ are edited either by the journal Editor, Neil Spiller, or by an invited Guest-Editor. Renowned for being at the leading edge of design and new technologies, △ also covers themes as diverse as architectural history, the environment, interior design, landscape architecture and urban design.

Provocative and pioneering, △ inspires theoretical, creative and technological advances. It questions the outcome of technical innovations as well as the far-reaching social, cultural and environmental challenges that present themselves today.

For further information on △ and purchasing single issues see:

https://onlinelibrary.wiley.com/journal/15542769

Individual backlist issues of △ are available as books for purchase starting at £29.99 / US$45.00

wiley.com

Americas
E: cs-journals@wiley.com
T: +1 877 762 2974

Europe, Middle East and Africa
E: cs-journals@wiley.com
T: +44 (0)18 6577 8315

Asia Pacific
E: cs-journals@wiley.com
T: +65 6511 8000

Japan (for Japanese-speaking support)
E: cs-japan@wiley.com
T: +65 6511 8010

Visit our Online Customer Help
available in 7 languages at
www.wileycustomerhelp.com/ask

Volume 93 No 4
ISBN 978-1-119-98396-5

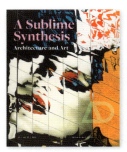

Volume 93 No 5
ISBN 978-1-394-17079-1

Volume 93 No 6
ISBN 978-1-394-16354-0

Volume 94 No 1
ISBN 978-1-394-17003-6

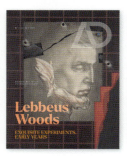

Volume 94 No 2
ISBN 978-1-119-98430-6

Volume 94 No 3
ISBN 978-1-394-19121-5